Dialogue for Writers

*Create Powerful Dialogue
in Fiction and Nonfiction*

Sammie Justesen

NorLightsPress.com
762 State Road 458
Bedford IN 47421

Printed in the United States of America
ISBN: 978-1-935254-90-4

Cover Design by Vorris Dee Justesen
Book Design by Nadene Carter

First printing, 2014

Contents

Introduction

THIS IS NOT AN ACADEMIC BOOK ON WRITING. I want *Dialogue for Writers* to be a fun, easy-going book to read, so relax and get comfortable. We don't mind a few coffee and chocolate stains on the pages.

I am not a professor with a string of titles after my name. Like you, I'm an author who has struggled with punctuation, plot, moral dilemmas, and the general angst of being creative. Here's my background:

Although my first career was critical care nursing, I always kept one foot in the publishing world. I began writing stories and poems in grade school, encouraged by doting parents and by seeing my work in the local newspaper. In the 1960s I attended Harvard for a time, lived in a Boston commune, and helped publish a weekly newspaper called The Avatar. In later years I worked as a clinical editor for medical publishers, and then I became a freelance editor. During that time I was fortunate to publish two novels and several nonfiction books. I opened a literary agency called Northern Lights Literary Services to help a group of my editing clients who couldn't find publishers. As an agent I truly began to understand the literary world as a business, from the publishing side. You might say the lights came on. In 2008, I became a publisher myself as part of NorLightsPress.com. What a long, strange trip it's been!

I am a born editor, intrigued by the nuts and bolts of writing. Perhaps because my mother was an English teacher, I've always had a passion for the red pencil. I reluctantly admit this to you: Even when reading the Bible, I find myself wanting to rearrange things.

Dialogue for Writers is written from my heart to yours. As a fellow author, I share your joy and your pain. I know the sweet agony of having one's hopes and dreams captured on a ream of white paper. I hope you'll delight in the journey as we explore dialogue—a facet of writing that touches every part of your work.

Why Dialogue?

All writers should love dialogue because it's the ultimate power trip. You put words into the mouths of other people. You decide what they say and how they say it. You're totally the boss—except when characters come to life and take over, and then you have even *more* fun. When you begin to master dialogue other things fall into place as well, including your skill as a writer.

I won't kid you: Mastery isn't easy. Theoretically, the task should be simple, since we spend much of our lives speaking or listening to others. But try recording a conversation, then reading it as dialogue. The resulting exchange will be lifeless and packed with clichés.

As you read this book you'll recognize the critical difference between real-life conversations and vivid dialogue. You will learn what dialogue can do and what it shouldn't do. You'll know when to add, when to cut, and how to edit. At the end of each chapter you'll find exercises to boost your confidence.

If you aspire to be published, know that dialogue is one of the first things agents and publishers notice in a manuscript. We can tell right away if you've failed to master the mechanics of speech.

Work that sets off the Weak Dialogue Alarm earns a one way trip to the dreaded slush pile. Agents and publishers keep one finger poised over the DELETE button on their email programs. Don't give them extra reasons to reject your work.

Many writers don't recognize the power of dialogue in certain genres, such as family histories, journals, poetry, and memoir. In Chapter Eleven You'll learn how dialogue can animate your personal stories and help create a legacy for your family.

You're about to learn the secrets of what makes dialogue work in every form of writing. Whether you're a seasoned author or a novice learning new skills, *Dialogue for Writers* will delight you with the enchanting world of dialogue.

Icons Used in This Book

Throughout the book I've included icons to highlight special information.

Do this to improve your writing.

Beware of this trap for writers

Chapter 1

Become a Master of Dialogue

FINDING VOICES FOR YOUR CHARACTERS is one of the most inspiring events you'll experience as a writer. The magic of dialogue can sweep readers away from their everyday lives, transporting them through time and space to a kingdom you've created, where things can disappear and appear again; where a single line or a sentence can change lives. As Frodo pronounced in *The Fellowship of the Ring:* "I will take the Ring, though I do not know the way."

This chapter presents an overview of how dialogue will enhance the stories you create. You'll find scenes in your work that beg to be told through the words of your characters. Perhaps your heroine finally tells her overbearing boss where to place his missing files. Or a father on his deathbed whispers to his grown son for the first and last time, "You did good, kid." A serial killer responds to voices inside his head while stalking his next victim. A police detective tells a mother her son was killed by a drunk driver. A sixteen year old lies to his parents about where he spent the night. Each of these events harnesses powerful emotions you can express through your characters' words and body language.

Dialogue Makes Your Pages Look Better

That's right: Dialogue on a page attracts attention because it breaks up blocks of prose and adds white space to the page, which pleases the eye. As I mentioned earlier, editors and agents will scan your work for dialogue. They like dialogue in general, but lame conversations can bring the whole manuscript down.

> Dialogue on a page attracts attention because it breaks up blocks of prose and adds white space to the page, which pleases the eye.

In well-constructed dialogue, your readers get to skip the boring small talk and enjoy conversations loaded with conflict and drama. Even the pauses between sentences are meaningful if you let characters reveal thoughts and feelings through their actions. When you want to convey information without drama, a few lines of narrative usually work best. But dialogue is the key when you need to show conflict, tension, details of a developing relationship, and changes in a character's thinking. All this, plus it's a quick read. For example, when a character reverses an opinion, which of the following appeals to your sense of drama?

Narrative statement: After reconsidering, he changed his mind.

Dialogue: "I'm here to apologize because I didn't look hard enough, until now."

A break-up conversation cries out for dialogue instead of narrative:

Narrative: This morning, Cassie picked up my phone and started thumbing through the messages. Too bad I forgot to delete everything. When she saw the pictures from Tasha it was all over for us.

Well, you can see where this is headed. Boring, right? How about dialogue instead?

"Who's this chick named Tasha on your phone? Oh, she sent you photos! And she's naked. And that's your sweater she's sitting on."

"Wait! I can explain."

"How could you do this to me? You arrogant, selfish creep. Get out of my life. I'm done with you."

"But..." The door slams shut (and so does her heart).

Okay, that's too melodramatic, but you get the idea. With dialogue the characters are handling things themselves while you (the writer) stay in the background.

Show it With Dialogue

The old adage "show don't tell" is so well known you probably learned it in grade school. Telling readers what they need to know is easy writing, but it comes across as a lecture. You leave no room for the magic that occurs when your writing sparks a reader's imagination. Well-crafted dialogue lets your readers discover things for themselves.

Telling readers what they need to know is easy writing, but it comes across as a lecture. You leave no room for the magic that occurs when your writing sparks a reader's imagination.

The sentence "She was a sexy woman" is not an appealing statement, because we want to know so much more. You might launch into a long description to show exactly why this woman is sexy, or you can have a character say the words:

"Wow, that chick is hot! Look at those long legs!" ...and so on.

Sure, for some situations you'll want to tell instead of showing. For example, you may decide to *tell* when:

- It isn't important to the story.
- The setting could be boring (someone sleeping).
- You need to be quick and efficient.
- The scene is a transition to something more interesting and exciting.

In the following dialogue, notice how Barbara Kingsolver reveals things about her characters:

> "You're not much of a talker," he said. "Most girls I know, they'll yap half the day about something they haven't done yet and might not get around to."
>
> "Well, then. I'm not most girls you know."
>
> ...They stood without speaking. She measured the silence by the cloud that crossed the sun, and by the two full wood-thrush songs that rang suddenly through the leaves and hung in the air between herself and this man...
>
> "All right if I just follow you for a while?" he asked politely.
>
> "No," she snapped. "That wouldn't suit me."

Here, dialogue moves the story, reveals character, and allows Kingsolver to describe the scenery. With only a few words, she reveals much about these characters. The man is pushing. The woman resists. We have conflict!

Through dialogue, you can explore a character's feelings by letting him speak emotional words. We express anger, fear, doubt, happiness, and every other human emotion in words. Conversely, dialogue might also convey lack of feelings or show characters who can't verbalize their thoughts. Either way—you win!

Dialogue Supplies Stealth Information

At the beginning of a piece you need to offer a certain amount of background information (backstory) that hooks your readers. This is where you need to get your mojo working. Over explaining has killed many a manuscript at birth, because novice writers tend to throw in huge blocks of text to explain each character's history, appearance, and attitudes.

///

Over explaining has killed many a manuscript at birth, because novice writers tend to throw in huge blocks of text to explain each character's history, appearance, and attitudes.

\\

Dialogue to the rescue! Conversation can help you avoid describing too much; it's a crafty way to provide information without putting your readers to sleep. You might call this stealth writing. When properly done, readers won't suspect you're giving them clues to the story ahead.

Here's how Lisa Gardner used dialogue to ease into Chapter Two of *Say Goodbye:*

> "We got a problem."
>
> "No kidding. Widespread production of methamphetamines, a middle class that keeps falling further and further behind, not to mention all the ruckus over global warming..."
>
> "No, no, no. A real problem."
>
> Kimberly sighed. They'd been working this crime scene for three days now. Long enough that she no longer noticed the smell of burning jet fuel and charcoaled bodies. She was cold, dehydrated, and had a stitch in her side. It would take a lot, in her opinion, to qualify as a real problem at this point.

Lisa continues in this vein, alternating terse, believable dialogue with descriptions of the scene and the main characters. She even uses humor:

"Better be good, Harold."

"Yep."

"If this is to show me some kind of rare moss or endangered grass species, I will kill you."

"I don't doubt it."

Lisa Gardner autographed a copy of this book for me and I couldn't put it down until I read the final page. Like many professionals, she uses dialogue to reveal her character's attitudes, physical attributes, and personal habits. Compare her snappy dialogue to this contrived conversation between a husband and wife:

"Your brother Fred is a doctor, and I think you should ask him about your stomach pain," Rachel said.

"Yes, but you know Fred and I haven't spoken for ten years because we didn't pay back the money we borrowed." Tom rubbed his belly and winced.

This stilted dialogue exists only to let the writer add background information—a subterfuge that irritates readers and makes characters sound like idiots. But, even this lame dialogue can be improved:

"Why don't you call Fred about those stomach pains?"

"Are you kidding? Right away he'll ask me about the ten thousand we own him."

"So what? Tell him you may have stomach cancer and we need help. It's time you two stopped acting like kids. Like every other doctor, he's rolling in money." Rachel held out the phone.

Use Dialogue to Foreshadow Events

Foreshadowing, a technique for planting information about future events, is especially vital for mystery and suspense novels. As the story reaches a climax, readers must believe events *had* to happen exactly as they unfold.

A good novel or screenplay contains clues most readers miss the first time around. The movie *The Sixth Sense* provides classic examples of foreshadowing. The director cleverly inserted hints and pointers most viewers didn't catch during the initial viewing.

Readers enjoy foreshadowing done with class and subtlety, because finding clues is fun and makes us feel clever.

Readers enjoy foreshadowing done with class and subtlety, because finding clues is fun and makes us feel clever. Careful use of this technique can add depth and interest to your writing.

Careful use of this technique can add depth and interest to your writing. On the first page of her book *White Oleander*, Janet Fitch uses a character's words to foreshadow a later tragedy:

> We could not sleep in the hot dry nights, my mother and I. I woke up at midnight to find her bed empty. I climbed to the roof and easily spotted her blond hair like a white flame in the light of the three-quarter moon.
>
> "Oleander time," she said. "Lovers who kill each other now will blame it on the wind."

And that's exactly what happens later in the story.

Dialogue and Character Driven Stories

Dialogue is especially important in stories that are driven more by characters than by plot. A story is character driven when the main characters' personalities, motivation, conflicts, strengths, and weaknesses create the action or plot. By contrast, a plot-driven story might center around a natural disaster or war scenes where the characters are secondary to external events. Plot driven dialogue tends to consist of phrases like, "Watch out!" or "Get him!"

Have you ever been watching a movie or reading a book when it hits you that something's wrong? When a clumsy line of dialogue destroys the image you created in your head, the entire spell is broken. "She wouldn't say that!" you tell yourself. The magic vanishes like smoke in the wind.

The movie *Changing Lanes (2002)* is a striking example of a character driven story. Two cars collide on an expressway and their drivers, who seem to have opposite personalities, engage in a brutal cycle of revenge. Characterization is so strong in this film that the plot unfolds in an unstoppable arc of violence. By the film's end we realize the social and economic differences between the men can't disguise the dark, angry nature they share. The dialogue is often terse and angry, much like the characters. Certainly, it reflects each character's motivation and internal conflicts.

Another example is *Castaway* (2000), starring Tom Hanks and his "friend" Wilson—a volleyball with whom the actor has long dialogues. This movie is a shining example of dialogue between a character and his imaginary friend. One of my favorite parts:

> "We might just make it. Did that ever cross your brain? Well, regardless I would rather take my chance out there on the ocean, than to stay here and die on this shithole island spending the rest of my life talking to a damn VOLLEYBALL."

Dialogue can make characters so believable they become cultural icons and live in our hearts for years. I'm betting you remember most of these dialogue fragments:

"Bah! Humbug!" (Ebeneezer Scrooge, of course!)

"Frankly, my dear, I don't give a damn." (Rhett Butler in *Gone With the Wind*)

"I'm going to make him an offer he can't refuse." (Vito Corleone in *The Godfather*)

"Here's looking at you, kid." (Rick Blaine in *Casablanca*)

"Go ahead, make my day." (Harry Callahan in *Sudden Impact*)

"Houston, we have a problem." (Jim Lovell in *Apollo 13*)

Notice how these single lines of dialogue sum up each character's personality and attitudes. That's what you're looking for as a writer. But well-crafted dialogue goes beyond witty exchanges and memorable lines. Magical dialogue can actually save a mediocre book or a dull movie.

Although some writers sweat over every speech they write while others have natural talent for dialogue, this is a skill you can master. The first step is to study the experts.

EXERCISES

Read a chapter of a novel or screenplay you especially like and look for the following:

1. How does the writer use dialogue to create tension?
2. Does the writer give each character a distinct voice? Find an example.
3. How does dialogue provide information about the characters?
4. How does the author provide background material through dialogue?
5. Does the writer use dialogue to foreshadow events? How?

Chapter 2

The Mechanics of Dialogue

READER ALERT: THIS MAY BE the most boring chapter in the book, but it can also keep you out of trouble when you run into thorny questions about grammar and punctuation. Too often our publishing firm receives manuscripts from writers who shrug off the rules of writing with lame excuses:

"I want to focus on story and characters, not punctuation."

"I use street dialogue and I don't need to punk it up with punctuation."

Or the ever popular, "I like to break the rules. That's who I am."

How about this one: "Let the editor fix my grammar after you give me that big advance on my work."

Trust me, publishers get so many submissions we don't take time to even read the ones with basic issues such as grammar and punctuation. Yes, sometimes it's okay to break the rules, but usually not with grammar and punctuation.

Publishers get so many submissions we don't take time to even read the ones with basic issues such as grammar and punctuation.

Incomplete sentences are sometimes okay. Even one word sentences. But a writer who's dedicated to the craft will invest in learning the basic tools of the trade. This is about respecting yourself and your readers. You'll also get better results when people see you're serious about your work.

What is Dialogue?

Dialogue is direct speech. Indirect speech, also called paraphrased speech, is not dialogue and does not require quotation marks.

Indirect speech: Rebecca said she was leaving.

Dialogue: "I'm leaving," Rebecca said.

Indirect speech: Tony yelled at us to watch out.

Dialogue: "Watch out! Tony shouted.

Who's Speaking?

Speaker tags, also called dialogue tags, denote who is speaking. *Said* is an excellent tag that fades into the background and is perfectly acceptable for repeated use.

Example: "I'm getting popcorn from the concession stand," Stan said.

Notice the speaker tags are *not* placed within quotation marks.

Example: "What happened here?" Chief Harris asked.

Internal Monologues

Thoughts a character doesn't speak aloud are referred to as internal monologues and do not require quotation marks. Traditionally, internal monologues were written in italics with no quotation marks: *I hope it doesn't rain,* Mark thought. The recent trend is to use internal monologues without special markings. Skillful writing tells us a character is thinking, not speaking aloud.

Example: I hope it doesn't rain, Mark thought.

Alternative: Mark hoped it wouldn't rain.

Example: Mark stared at the dark clouds on the horizon. I hope it doesn't rain. I'll look like a drowned rat for my job interview.

Commas

Use a comma instead of a period to set off speaker tags—the words immediately following a speech, such as *he said* or *she replied*. The period goes at the end of the speaker tag.

Correct: "I won't do it," he said.

Incorrect: "I won't do it", he said.

Incorrect: "I won't do it," He said.

Notice the comma comes before the quotation mark, not after. Do not capitalize the first word of the speaker tag.

Question Marks and Exclamation Points

When quoted words end with a question mark or an exclamation point, use that punctuation even if explanatory words follow.

Correct: "I won't do it!" he shouted.

Incorrect: "I won't do it"! he shouted.

Incorrect: "I won't do it," he shouted!

Correct: "Is it morning yet?" she asked.

The question mark or exclamation point goes before the quotation marks and is never positioned after the speaker tag. Don't capitalize the first word of the speaker tag.

Broken-off Speech

People interrupt one another during conversations, and sometimes a speaker's words fade out as his attention wanders. Two types of punctuation show broken-off speech: the ellipsis and the dash.

Ellipsis: "I suppose that a good idea... I don't know. "Okay..."

Dash: Wow, look at that tyrannosaurus rex! I wonder—"

Use a dash within a sentence to emphasize information and a shift in tone—as I do here—or at the end of a quote to indicate someone is hesitating. This is different from the ellipsis, which should only be used to show dialogue that trails off and will probably start again.

Dashes are more complicated than you'd expect, because they come in two varieties: the en dash and the em dash. An en dash is slightly longer than a hypen (-), but shorter than the em dash. An en dash is the width of the letter "N," while an em dash is as wide as the letter "M." Use the en dash to indicate "through" in date and numbers (1 through 5 written as 1 – 5).

Typewriter and computer keyboards don't contain keys for either em or en dashes, but most word processing software programs will automatically turn two hyphens into an em dash if you correctly leave no space before or after them.

Do you have trouble placing a dash at the end of a character's speech because your computer wants to turn your quotation mark the wrong way? For example, with this phrase: Bill said, "I wonder if she'll—" My word processing program inserts backwards quotation marks after the dash. To correct this, insert a letter (any letter) after the dash: Bill said, "I wonder if she'll—g" Now delete the "g" and you're left with an em dash and the proper quotation mark: Bill said, "I wonder if she'll—"

I'm sure there's an easier solution, but I have yet to find it.

Paragraphs

Using paragraphs can be tricky, because with dialogue each speaker gets a new paragraph, no matter how short the speech.

"Why are we even negotiating with this guy?" Frank said.

"Don't ask questions; just deliver the message." Frank stalked away, heading for the car.

If a speaker's words change direction and you need a second paragraph for the same speech, add quotation marks at the beginning of each paragraph, but at the end of *only* the last paragraph.

"Get away from here you rotten kids! If I ever see you in my yard again I'll wail the tar outta ya. *(no quotation marks here)*

"I hope those little urchins didn't hurt you, Ma'am." He bowed to Lily.

Each speaker gets his own paragraph, even if the speech is only one word:

"No!" Rachel shouted.

"Why not?" Bill asked.

Placing dialogue inside a paragraph is the right thing to do when you're quoting someone. For example,

"I don't give a flip about punctuation," one writer told me.

If I answer him, the response needs a new paragraph.

"No problem. I hope you find another publisher," I responded.

A Quote Within a Quote

What happens when a character who's speaking quotes someone else or talks about his own thoughts? In that case, you add a single quotation mark within the paragraph. A quote within a quote calls for single quotation marks—and that's the only time you use them. Sometimes you'll need to use three quote marks at the end of a sentence; one for the quote within a quote, and two for the dialogue. Confused? Read these examples:

"I think Wordsworth phrased it best when he said, 'The budding rose above the rose full grown.'" James smiled and held out a yellow rose.

Notice the end of this speech required three quotation marks —one for the quote within a quote, plus a regular quotation mark to end the dialogue line. Here's a different type of quote within a quote from *Trunk Music*, by Michael Connelly:

"You know, Lucky keeps making noises about being set up. He, of course, thinks it's us putting him in the frame and I know that's bull. But I keep thinking, 'What if there is a frame?' I mean, I have to admit that him keeping that gun is hard to figure, though I've seen even dumber moves in my time."

To complicate matters, what if one of your characters decides to quote several lines of poetry? In this case, you separate the poetry from the text with space and an indentation. Do not add quotation marks.

James fell to his knees before her and opened the slender red book he'd carried to the garden. "I hope you like Emily Dickinson, my dear. This is a favorite of mine:

> I more than once at Noon
> Have passed, I thought, a whiplash
> Unbraiding in the Sun
> When stopping to secure it
> It wrinkled, and was gone—

What do you think?" he asked

Is your head spinning from all this dialogue and punctuation? Don't worry. Writing correct dialogue will soon become second nature.

EXERCISES

Punctuate and correct the following:
1. Oars? Safety chain? Distress flares? Do you have a safety chain for your motor? Fred asked. No said Sam.
2. I wonder if Steven made it to work on time, Marcia thought.
3. Get out of my life she shouted.
4. I wonder if Paul said before he slammed on the brakes.
5. Joyce rubbed her temples and said Was it Shakespeare who said, To be or not to be? Losing your memory is no fun, she thought.

ANSWERS

1. "Oars? Safety chain? Distress flares? Do you have a safety chain for your motor?" Fred asked.
   "No," said Sam.
2. No quotation marks. I wonder if Steven made it to work on time, Marcia thought.
3. "Get out of my life!" she shouted.
4. "I wonder if—" Paul said before he slammed on the brakes.
5. Joyce rubbed her temples and said, "Was it Shakespeare or Walt Whitman who said, 'To be or not to be?'" Losing your memory is no fun, she thought.

Chapter Three

The Illusion of Dialogue

DIALOGUE MAGIC BEGINS WHEN A writer transforms everyday speech into dramatic, sparkling conversation.

The best dialogue truly is an illusion. As a writer, you want to *suggest* the way people speak, not copy their exact words. Have you ever recorded a conversation and then transcribed it to paper? If so, then you know exactly what I mean: Most people are verbally challenged. They mumble, search for the right words, and blurt out the wrong things. They use the same phrases too many times and get lazy with jargon (like using the word *like* at the beginning of each sentence or dropping f-bombs after every other word).

The enchantment begins when you learn to make conversations sound natural, while at the same time, eliminating the boring re-petition of normal speech. Fictional dialogue should focus on highlights—the emotional peaks. The best dialogue becomes part of the action: it moves the story along, reveals character, and provides information. Eventually, you'll develop an ear for the nuances of dialogue. You can speed this process by tuning in to conversations wherever you go—school, restaurants, busses, parks, and your own

The best dialogue truly is an illusion. As a writer, you want to suggest the way people speak, not copy their exact words.

home. Later, try writing parts of the conversations; decide what to keep, which parts to leave out, and try arranging the whole thing into a compelling block of text. You may find yourself conjuring up enchanting new characters who speak dialogue like this:

Suppose your heroine (Rita) is lunching with her daughter at the corner restaurant. The daughter (Erin) desperately needs a loan. Before she hits her mother up for the money, Erin will devote half an hour to small talk, asking about Rita's job at the bank, bonding with her, and gradually working money problems into the conversation. Your readers don't need to hear this tedious small talk, although the fact that it occurs is relevant to the story. Nor do they need to know how Rita takes her coffee or how many times Erin sprinkles salt on her food. Your job as a writer is to find the essence of this conversation while adding enough detail to make it realistic.

Your job as a writer is to find the essence of this conversation while adding enough detail to make it realistic.

After two cups of coffee and half an hour of small talk, Rita got down to business. "Mom, my car payment was due last week and I'm short on cash until I find another job. Maybe you could help me out?"

"I wondered why you asked me to lunch." Rita crooked her finger at the waiter and pointed to her water glass. "Now I know."

"I wanted to see you." Erin stuck out her lower lip.

Rita laughed. "I'm your mother. You can't fool me, sweet-heart."

"Okay, I'm desperate. Want to hear me beg?"

Erin did look frightened, and Rita saw she'd been chewing her nails again. Her right thumbnail was ragged, bitten down to the quick. Heaving an exaggerated sigh, Rita dug through her purse and produced a checkbook. "How much do you need this time?"

In real life, Erin would smooth things over with more small talk and Rita would respond in kind. Then they'd pay the bill, discuss the tip, stand up, and leave the restaurant. Since most of these activities don't advance the story, there's no need to dramatize them.

Introductions are also a challenge for novice writers. Suppose Rita's colleague Mr. French appears in the restaurant and must be introduced to Erin:

"Erin, I'd like you to meet Mr. French, who works with me at the bank."

Erin extended her hand. "Nice to meet you," she said.

"I've seen a photo of you on your mother's desk," Mr. French said.

"Great." Erin returned her gaze to the dessert menu.

As a reader, did this exchange between Erin and Mr. French quicken your pulse?

Although it happens every day in real life, this detailed small talk is tedious and unnecessary. If this meeting is relevant, just write, "Rita introduced Erin to Mr. French, a teller from the bank." Then get on with the story.

On the other hand, what if Rita is having an affair with Mr. French (who is married) and is afraid Erin will pick up on it? Now you have serious tension. Or, you might use poor Mr. French as a pawn to reveal competition between mother and daughter. Is Erin rude to her mother's colleague? Does Rita flirt with Mr. French, who's fifteen years her junior? Perhaps Mr. French is attentive to Erin and Rita feels a pang of jealousy. If you bring Mr. French into your story, he shouldn't come empty handed. Make him add tension, conflict, or suspense.

Conflict, Tension, or Suspense

Every scene in your novel or screenplay should be animated by conflict, tension, or suspense. Tension doesn't always imply argument or conflict; it may arise from unexpressed feelings and other human angst. Open to a page in any well written book and you'll find tension. For example, here are three random lines from *The Last Child* by John Hart:

> "I need you to show me."
>
> "Aw, man." Steve looked up at the rain. "You're going to get me wet *and* fired." Nobody laughed.
>
> "Now," Hunt said.
>
> …Yoakum's hand fell on Hunt's shoulder. "Backup?" He held out his radio.
>
> "We're not waiting."
>
> "Good." Yoakum put the radio in his pocket and racked the slide on his weapon. "I hate waits."

Whatever trouble these men are facing, John Hart ramps up the story by having them charge forward without waiting for backup. (Do heroes *ever* wait for backup?)

Whether the conflict is internal or external, as author Elizabeth Bowen points out "The writer must know, always, what the scene is trying to accomplish. If not, the characters will just run on, and the scene will lose the dynamic tension of the big picture, the 'aboutness' of the novel."

Dialogue is indeed a powerful tool at your disposal. Elizabeth Bowen summarized the following attributes:

1. Dialogue should be brief.
2. It should add to the reader's present knowledge.
3. It should eliminate the routine exchanges of ordinary conversation.
4. It should convey a sense of spontaneity, but eliminate the repetitiveness of real talk.
5. It should keep the story moving forward.
6. It should be revelatory of the speaker's character, both directly and indirectly.
7. It should show the relationships among people.

Bowen adds, "Short of a small range of physical acts—a fight, a murder, love-making—dialogue is the most vigorous and interaction of which characters in a novel are capable. Speech is what the characters do to each other."

Sol Stein, novelist, editor, and teachers advises that, "Dialogue is a foreign language, different from whatever language a writer has grown up using. It can make people unknown to the writer cry, laugh, and believe lies in seconds. It is succinct, can carry a great weight of meaning in few words, and above all, it is adversarial. That doesn't mean shouting. Adverserial dialogue can be subtle."

You'll be halfway there with dialogue if you remember to give each character a personal agenda and a singular way of responding to conflict and tension.

You'll be halfway there with dialogue if you remember to give each character a personal agenda and a singular way of responding to conflict and tension.

Continue the Illusion with Fragments

If you've ever longed to get away with writing incomplete sentences, here's your chance. In real life, people use short, choppy sentences. Don't be afraid to let sentence fragments add a natural touch to your dialogue. Fragments help writers create rhythm and drama during high tension or rushed scenes. Comic books and graphic novels are perfect example of this dialogue:

> "Help ... me ... Not much timmme..."
> "Desperate ... Gotta get help..."
> "Superman ... Don't understand ... Must tell you..."
> "Sue ... in danger ... Whole world ... epidemic."

Obviously someone got carried away with the elipses (dots) in this example from a Superman comic. I'm not recommending you write this way all the time, but comics can be a fun place to study dialogue.

Here's a fragmented conversation from *Still Life with Murder* by P.B. Ryan:

> "Even the best lawyer can't work miracles," she said. "Especially when their clients are as difficult as—"
> "It doesn't matter!" He wheeled to face her, that vein rising on his forehead, his eyes red-rimmed.
> "It doesn't matter how difficult he is. He's my friend, the only real friend I have left, and I can't ... I can't..."

"You're upset because you've been drinking, she said evenly. "But we haven't exhausted all our options. When you're more yourself, we'll talk about—"

"More myself?" He laughed, but his eyes shone damply.

The conversation sounds authentic; even in this brief segment P.B. Ryan maintains each character's agenda. It's no surprise later in the book when one of these characters self-destructs.

Real People Speak with Contractions.

I can't emphasize enough the importance of heeding this simple rule: *Use contractions with your dialogue.* Hardly anyone speaks formally in this day and age, so if you're writing modern conversation, you need to use the contracted form of verbs.

I can't emphasize enough the importance of heeding this simple rule: *Use contractions with your dialogue.*

Everyday speech is quick and sloppy; therefore, the best writers use contractions in dialogue without thinking twice. Writing without contractions is all too common among fledgling writers who struggle to iron out every possible wrinkle in their prose. Here's an example of a stilted sentence without contractions:

"Mother, I will not walk to school today because is it raining. My hair will be ruined."

Better: "Mom, I can't believe you expect me to walk in the rain! What about my hair?"

A character who's foreign to the English language may speak more formally. Even so, readers won't like your conversations if you don't use at least some contractions.

What about historical fiction? Since we have no actual recorded speech from early periods, who can say for sure? Written dialogue was usually formal. As *Merriam-Webster's Dictionary of English Usage* explains,

> *Won't* was among the contracted and truncated forms that Joseph Addison attacked in *The Spectator* on 4 August 1711. It seems to have been under something of a cloud, as far as the right-thinkers were concerned, for more than a century afterward. This did not, of course, interfere with its employment, and it was common enough to enjoy the distinction of being damned in the same breath as *ain't* in an address delivered before the Newburyport (Mass.) Female High School in December 1846. The speaker termed both "absolutely vulgar."

> However, it's likely humans have abbreviated their conversations ever since we invented language. While you may have good reasons for using formal speech in historical writing, your readers won't care. They want a book (or story, or biography) that's entertaining and interesting to read. The best compromise is to provide an illusion of formality by having the characters use a few formal phrases here and there, sprinkled lightly. Of course you'll also use actual phrases and language from the time period.

Lightning in a Bottle

In powerful dialogue, every sentence carries energy and has a purpose. Delete every line of dialogue that doesn't fit this rule, and don't be tempted to insert extra dialogue to take up space. Empty dialogue includes dozens of throw-away phrases we use in real life, such as:

"What's happening, man?" (or "What up, bro?")

"How've you been?"

"Can you tell me..."

"Do you mind if..."

"Thanks."

"You're welcome."

//
In powerful dialogue, every sentence carries energy and has a purpose. Delete every line of dialogue that doesn't fit this rule.
\\

Sure, this is how real people speak, but it makes tedious reading. Try cutting these exchanges from your manuscript to make conversations more exciting. Here's an example of how summarizing can help you cut to the heart of a scene:

> We met in the park and Susan linked her arm through mine the way she always did. I bent slightly toward her, hoping to catch the scent of her shampoo. Walking the paths, we chatted about her job, my next trip, and the latest movie playing at the theatre. Nothing serious, keeping it light. Then everything changed.
>
> "I think I've fallen in love with someone at work," she said.

There it is! That last sentence is lightening in a bottle. To find it, the writer omitted a full page of details and idle chatter. I know this, because I was the writer. And don't think I enjoyed deleting my hard work. But I had to admit the details were distracting.

"What do readers *need* to know?" I asked myself. "Where's the juicy part?" I ended up with only a few lines, but I believe readers will be happy with this kind of dialogue. I kept the part where the lightening leaves the jar.

EXERCISES

1. Using dialogue, write a scene about a situation that happened to you—a job interview, an annoying or frightening encounter with a stranger, getting a traffic ticket. You chose the scenario. Experiment by writing the scene with detail, and then try cutting it to the bare bones. Which version do you like best?

2. Write a scene describing an argument or discussion you've witnessed (real or imagined). Narrate the scene yourself, but let others provide the entire dialogue. Here's a sample opening:

   > I hid in my usual spot on the stairway and listened to the argument that started the second Dad opened the front door.
   >
   > "Where's your damn paycheck?" Ma shouted.

3. Remember a conversation you recently overheard or took part in. Rewrite the dialogue to make it more lively and interesting.

Chapter Four

Dialect, Accents, and Language

REGIONAL ACCENTS AND SPEECH PATTERNS can easily overwhelm your writing and ruin a well-crafted story. On the other hand, this type of dialogue can also make your writing more authentic. Most people love reading about places we've never lived, new cultures, odd dialects, and eccentric characters.

Does your heritage include a particular dialect, language, or speech pattern? If so, you should be able to use it with ease in your writing. But no matter what speech patterns you learned during childhood, as a serious writer you'll eventually need to use voices (dialect, slang, and accents) that differ from your own. Dozens of movies and books feature dueling dialects. The stuffy, aristocratic British accent is well known and widely used ("I say, old chap!"). And who doesn't love the Cockney dialect ("Here! What are you sniggering at?")

In the film *Pretty Woman*, we watched a mouthy Los Angeles hooker fall in love with a proper New York businessman. *Good Will Hunting* featured a South Boston punk at Harvard. A more recent film, *The Best Exotic Marigold Hotel,* highlights a group of British retirees who outsource their retirement—along with cultural prejudices—to India. ("One has read one's Kipling" is a classic line). This film offers an elegant example of how language and communication issues build characterization and move the plot.

If you choose to write about someone with a particular dialect, you'd be wise to learn about the underlying culture before you start putting words into someone's mouth.

If you choose to write about someone with a particular dialect, you'd be wise to learn about the underlying culture before you start putting words into someone's mouth.

The Scoop on Dialect and Accents

Dialect is a form of a language peculiar to a specific region or cultural group. A basic language, such as English, French, German, or Arabic can have dozens of dialects. In France, a person raised in Paris might speak a different dialect than someone born in the French countryside.

If you want to have serious fun with American dialects, check out the work of Joshua Katz, a graduate student in statistics at North Carolina State University. As a project for one of his classes, Katz produced a study called "Beyond Soda, Pop, or Coke" and illustrated his findings with a fascinating series of U.S. dialect maps. When the colorful maps went viral on the Internet, the host had to create a dedicated cluster to accommodate heavy traffic: [http://spark.rstudio.com/jkatz/SurveyMaps] View further information at: [http://www4.ncsu.edu/-jakatz2/project-dialect.html] The new page includes a survey you can take to identify your own dialect.

Dialect reflects the vocabulary and usage of a specific group of people, such as calling a carbonated soft drink soda, pop, or coke. An accent is the way words are pronounced. Someone from Germany might speak English with a foreign accent, and you may want to show this in dialogue.

//
Dialect reflects the vocabulary and usage of a specific group of people. An accent is the way words are pronounced.
\\

Slang and Jargon

You'll be tempted to use slang and jargon in your dialogue. Popular slang is constantly being reinvented by the young and propagated by social media. New expressions evolve and grow stale every week as people reshape the English language. And here lies the problem with using slang in your work: It can date your writing and make you seem hopelessly un-hip. Dude, that's bad. Or rad. Or something.

You can see why it's best to be careful with slang and jargon in your dialogue, unless you purposefully want to place your characters in a certain era. Perhaps your character is mired in the 1960s, like The Dude in the Coen brother's film *The Big Lebowski.* You can play around with hipster culture of the 1950s, prison slang, street slang ... the possibilities are endless. But how far should you go?

Too much of a good thing

Dialect, slang, and accents should give your readers just an impression of something different—like a whiff of perfume in the air. Don't choke them with it. Heavy dialect or slang is guaranteed to annoy. Yes, your characters should all sound different, not like cardboard cutouts. But if you over-do regional speech, readers lose the flow while stumbling over unfamiliar words and phrases.

Dialect, slang, and accents should give your readers just an impression of something different—like a whiff of perfume in the air. Don't choke them with it.

Complex dialogue filled with apostrophes confuses people, and they begin skipping parts of the story. Here's a classic example of unreadable dialogue from *Uncle Tom's Cabin* by Harriet Beecher Stowe:

> "S'pose we must be resigned; but oh Lord! How ken I? If I know'd anything whar you's goin', or how they'd sarve you! Missis says she'll try and 'deem ye, in a year or two, but Lor! Nobody never comes up that goes down thar! They kills 'em! I've hearn 'em tell how dey works 'em up on de mar plantations."

Dialogue should be music to our eyes, with its own rhythm and style. You can't achieve this by using a mishmash of contractions and misspelled words. If your readers have never actually heard the dialect you're using (Cajun, Spanish, Black urban, etc.), will they truly be able to learn it from your writing? Many teachers and writers would say no.

The secret formula revealed

How can writers show dialogue and accents without burdening the story? The answer is simple: you achieve better results by using a few key phrases and adding a smidgen of unusual dialect, especially if you make these words specific to one character. Here's an example of British English from *Night Frost* by R. D. Wingfield:

> Her eyes fluttered, then opened. She seemed unable to focus. Frost knelt beside her.

"What happened, love? Who did it?" He turned his head away as the stale gin fumes hit him.

"I fell down the bleeding stairs," she said.

Notice how Frost shows us the characters are British by using two simple words: *love* and *bleeding*. Anne Perry also portrays British English, and her characters speak without heavy dialect. However, she gives minor characters, such as this shopkeeper, more leeway:

The man leaned over the counter and pointed leftwards, waving his arm. "About half a mile up that way, and one street over. Can't miss it. Up towards Mrs. Anderson's, it is. But you'd know that, knowing Mrs. Gardiner an' all."

Robert Dugoni's character Melda has a different background, shown by her intonation:

Melda stood on the landing holding a bundle of envelopes. "I bring for you your mail, Mr. David. This time, it is not too much. Just the bills and the junk."

Back to the British Isles, where James Herriot does a masterful rendition of the rural British accent in his book *All Creatures Great and Small*. Here, a few well-placed words and apostrophes portray this character's dialect without going over the top:

"And how long have you been qualified, may I ask?"

"Oh, about seven months."

"Seven months!" Uncle smiled indulgently, tamped down his tobacco and blew out a cloud of rank, blue smoke. "Well, there's nowt like a bit of experience, as I always says. Mr. Broomfield's been doing my work now for over ten years and he really knows what he's about. No, you can 'ave your book learning. Give me experience any time."

This same technique works with New York, Creole, southern, and every other dialect. Sprinkle a few words into your dialogue and let the reader's imagination take it from there. Beware of letting dialect define a character. You still need character traits and a personality for each person in your story; otherwise they become stereotypes of a race, class, or region.

Beware of letting dialect define a character. You still need character traits and a personality for each person in your story; otherwise they become stereotypes of a race, class, or region.

Science Fiction and Fantasy

In science fiction you may be describing not only a foreign culture, but an alien culture. The challenge is to create new words that make sense, while sounding a bit exotic. Before writing dialogue, you'll need a clear picture of the society you've created and how the characters (human and otherwise) behave. You don't want to rehash those early films where every society in the universe spoke like white middle class Americans.

Don't clutter science fiction dialogue with words and phrases your readers won't understand. Introduce new concepts one at a time and keep things relatively simple. Made-up words should be used several times so readers will remember them. It helps if they are new, yet familiar, at the same time—as in the following excerpt.

Verbal styles should vary with different cultures and species. Also, your characters' internal dialogue must follow the cultural mindset you've established. In this except from *The Skies of Pern*, by Anne McCaffrey, a young man named F'lessan exchanges mental dialogue with his dragon:

> *You protect Hunshu. I like being there very much,* said his dragon, Golanth, from where he had steeled himself in the hot noontime sun among the dragons who had brought their riders to Landing's Turnover festivities. *Good sunning places, clear water, and many fat herdbeasts.*
>
> F'lessan stuffed his riding gloves into the Turnover gift of a fine carisak, giving the wide cuffs a good push; the new wher-hide leather was stiff, despite the good oiling he had given it yesterday evening. The carisak had been presented to him by Lessa and F'lar. He rarely thought of them as "mother" or "father:" they were his Weyrleaders, and that was more relevant... As F'lessan grew up and saw how easygoing life was in a weyr, and the conformity required of children in the holds, he was as glad he'd been weyrbred.

While eavesdropping on F'lessan's thoughts, we easily deduce the meanings of the new words McCaffey created—herdbeasts, carisak, and weyr. Notice how many times she used the word weyr in this paragraph. It's an important concept in the book.

Science fiction dialogue gives you the opportunity to create wonderfully complex characters who speak with animals, commune with aliens, and have an entirely different mind-set than normal earthlings. But you still need to follow the basic rules of writing.

Historical Fiction

Historical fiction is a balancing act; you want the characters to sound authentic without being weighed down by stilted language. Again, you should use the secret formula by inserting only measured amounts of historical language and background.

Of course you'll try to avoid modern slang and phrases, but this can be trickier than you imagine. I recommend having someone you trust review your work for discrepancies.

You'll need reference books and research to get it right. Books are available from Penguin Publishers, including *The Penguin Dictionary of Historical Slang*. Random House publishes a two-volume series called *The Random House Historical Dictionary of American Slang*.

You must also learn the mind-set and cultural attitudes of the period you're representing. How would children address their elders? What role did women have in society? How did people spend their time? How did the ruling classes differ from the lower classes? You don't want to create a poorly disguised version of modern times coated with a veneer of historical facts.

For historical dialogue, you must also learn the mind-set and cultural attitudes of the period you're representing. You don't want to create a poorly disguised version of modern times coated with a veneer of historical facts.

Primary sources are some of the best research materials you can use. Old diaries and journals are rich with language and historical detail. Old newspapers are available in libraries or online. Sometimes you'll find entire conversations recorded, which can be invaluable. Pay special attention to the advertisements; they can tell you a lot about culture, fads, and habits.

Foreign accents

Here's another challenge for writers: a character who speaks a foreign language at times or speaks English with a distinct accent. Some authors solve this problem by writing the character's speeches in English, them repeating them in the second language, or vice versa: He shook his head. "Je ne sais pas, ma cherie. That I do not know."

This device is effective for minor characters who make a brief appearance, but it becomes tiresome when used throughout a book. Another technique is to insert occasional foreign phrases into the character's speech: "Bonjour," he said. "I am Marcel de Becque." This too becomes annoying when overdone.

Many writers successfully use gestures and body language to impart a foreign flavor to their characters. Greg Iles in *Dead Sleep*:

De Becque makes a very French gesture with his open hands, which I translate as *Some things we must accept without explanation*.

No need to constantly show us your character is from a different culture; it's more effective to insert an occasional reminder—a simple phrase or gesture that indicates foreignness. Think of foreign accents as an exotic spice that can ruin the dish if overused.

No need to constantly show us your character is from a different culture; it's more effective to insert an occasional reminder—a simple phrase or gesture that indicates foreignness.

Vulgar language and political correctness

In our culture four letter words have almost lost their power. Even the term *vulgar language* sounds old fashioned, because almost nothing is taboo these days. Consider your audience as you write, and also think about how you want to be viewed as a writer. Do you want parents to hide your book from the kids? Would your mother be ashamed to show it to her book club?

Since the original version of my dialogue book, publishers have begun selling books with titles such as

Sh*t My Dad Says

A**holes Finish First

Go the F**k to Sleep

Another Bull**** Night in Suck City.

Most publishers won't print books with profanity on the covers, but the inside is a different story. One could argue that violence and explicit sex do as much damage as naughty words. In the end, it's your choice, but keep in mind that using words for shock value is lazy writing.

Some writers believe avoiding foul language results in a story that isn't honest and doesn't reflect a true world. They go overboard in portraying reality by tossing the F-bomb into every conversation. This may be realistic, but it's also boring. Don't assume you're building a strong character by having him use the same words in every speech. A few swear words scattered here and there will portray a character as tough and street-wise.

When I was a literary agent, an editor I hoped to work with responded with a scathing email because a memoir I sent her contained two swear words on the first page. She hated it. The author promised to purge all the "F bombs," but he was too late. She refused to consider the book for publication. This wasn't a Christian publisher—just an editor with high standards, and I learned a lesson I won't soon forget.

Perhaps you agree with that editor. Why propagate vulgarity and force it on your readers? Your audience may contain people who won't watch a movie or read a book containing vulgar words. Your readers may have children who'll pick up the book and flip through it.

In his book *On Writing*, Stephen King reports getting several letters a week accusing him of being "foul-mouthed, bigoted, homophobic, murderous, frivolous, or downright psychopathic."

King adds, "I grew up as part of America's lower middle class, and they're the people I can write about with the most honesty and knowledge. It means they say shit more often than sugar when they bang their thumbs, but I've made my peace with that."

On the other hand, are you contributing to the debasement of our culture by using profane and obscene words? Are you taking the easy way out? Four letter words won't scare every publisher away from your work, but why not learn to portray evil without using crass language?

Are you taking the easy way out? Four letter words won't scare every publisher away from your work, but why not learn to portray evil without using crass language?

Each regional dialect has colorful words that convey derision without actually swearing. William Shakespeare was a master at delivering heinous insults without using profanity:

- Thou art a boil, a plague sore, an embossed carbuncle in my corrupted blood.
- From the extremist upward of thy head to the descent and dust beneath thy foot, a most toad spotted traitor.
- He's a most notable coward, an infinite and endless liar, an hourly promise breaker, the owner of not one good quality.

The type of language your characters use is your choice. But never forget who'll be reading your book or watching the movie.

EXERCISES:

1. Select a particular dialect that interests you and develop a character who will speak that dialect. Determine his history, educational background, and temperament.

2. Write a scene in which this character loses something important and expresses strong emotion. What regional words does he use?

3. Write a mental dialogue between a human and an animal.

4. Construct a dialogue between an American and someone who speaks broken English.

Read a screenplay or watch a movie that contains dialect. Note how the writer handles regional speech. Eavesdrop in a different neighborhood and listen for regional speech. What gestures and body language accompany words?

Chapter Five
Tags, Adverbs, and Participles

Dialogue Tags

DIALOGUE TAGS (used to denote who's speaking) can be a puzzle for writers, who pose such questions as: "Should every speech be tagged?" and "How many times should I use 'He said' and 'She said' on a single page?"

Writers often derail perfectly good stories by attempting to replace the word *said* with exotic substitutes. Characters bellow, snicker, chortle, demand, query, bark, chirp, and gasp. I admit it—I've been there.

///
Writers often derail perfectly good stories by attempting to replace the word *said* with exotic substitutes.
\\\

My early writing included horrible dialogue tags, but I soon learned that clumsy substitutes for *said* interrupt the flow of prose, distract readers, and become offensive after a few pages. Here's an example of dialogue burdened by excess tags:

> "Please help me," Sandy pleaded.
>
> "What's wrong with you now, woman?" Jack growled menacingly.
>
> "I'm about to drop these groceries. Can't you take one of the bags?" she begged.
>
> "You lift weights at the gym three times a week and still can't manage a few groceries?" Jack snarled. Maybe I should cancel our membership," he barked.

We immediately recognize Jack as a first class jerk. Do we need to hear him growl and bark at Sandy? Describing his actions shows his feelings more clearly than using lame dialogue tags:

> "Please help me!" Sandy stumbled on the bottom step, nearly losing her grip on the brown paper sack in her arms. The plastic bag dangling from her wrist banged against the banister.
>
> "What's wrong with you, woman?" Jack paused on the top step, glaring down at her.
>
> "I'm about to drop these groceries. Can't you take one of the bags?"
>
> He kept walking, but shouted back, "You lift weights at the gym three times a week and still can't manage a few groceries? Maybe I should cancel our membership."

Overblown dialogue tags break the cardinal rule in fiction: show, don't tell. In the second example above, Sandy and Jack 's words and actions *show* us how they're feeling; we don't need the writer telling us with dialogue tags.

Inexperienced writers tend to use exotic dialogue tags for several reasons:

- They haven't developed an ear, or they don't read their work aloud. Therefore, they don't realize how jolting these substitutes are for the reader.
- They think using vivid dialogue tags will make the story more exciting and help describe the characters.
- They fear readers won't understand a character's feelings and tone of voice without heavy-handed dialogue tags.
- In an effort to sound clever and literary, they use the thesaurus to find colorful substitutes for the word *said*.

Always keep in mind that your character's words are the most important element in dialogue, not the tags following the words. You will see novels in print with lurid dialogue tags, especially in the romance genre. Unfortunately, such tags don't prevent a book from being published. They do "tag" an author who's inexperienced or inept.

Another point to remember is that tags express verbalization. The words laughed, smiled, pouted, shrugged, snarled, and growled do not denote speech. If Jack actually snarled and barked at Sandy in the above conversation, he wasn't speaking. Words that do express verbalization include said, answered, replied, shouted, and whispered. Place a list of acceptable dialogue tags in your writing notebook so you won't have characters who pout, chortle, grin, and frown while they're trying to speak.

Here's the ultimate formula for dialogue tags: Keep it simple. Concentrate on the words your characters speak and worry about dialogue tags later. If your dialogue is well written, readers will barely notice the word *said*.

//
Here's the ultimate formula for dialogue tags: Keep it simple. If your dialogue is well written, readers will barely notice the word *said*.
\\

I challenge you to look through your writing and try to eliminate dialogue tags. You may be surprised by how many of these little distractions you can delete. This works especially well during short, crisp exchanges between two characters. You know your writing is strong when readers can follow the dialogue without any speaker tags. Here's a telephone conversation from Stephen White's novel *The Program*:

> He was dismissive. "You have an idea where we could go?"
>
> "Sure, there're some places we could go from my house. Do you know where I live?"
>
> "I'm guessing Boulder."
>
> "County, not the city. It's actually a little east, near the scenic overlook on 36."
>
> "Morbul Bismarck neighborhood. I'll throw my bike in the back of the truck. Give me directions."
>
> Alan did.
>
> Ron said, "I can be there by nine."
>
> "Then I guess I'll see you then."

In this example it's easy to tell which character is speaking, yet White placed only one dialogue tag in the conversation. The two men don't like one another, so their speech lacks warmth. Tacking on dialogue tags would've been distracting and slowed the scene's flow. Let's see how this dialogue would look with tags added:

> He was dismissive. "You have an idea where we could go?" he asked.
>
> "Sure, there're some places we could go from my house," Alex said. "Do you know where I live?"
>
> "I'm guessing Boulder," Ron said.
>
> "County, not the city. It's actually a little east, near the scenic overlook on 36," Alex said.

"Morbul Bismarck neighborhood," Ron said. "I'll throw my bike in the back of the truck. Give me directions."

Alan did.

Ron said, "I can be there by nine."

"Then I guess I'll see you then," Alex said.

Don't you like the scene better without dialogue tags? The important thing is to vary your writing so that no scene contains dialogue tags after every speech, and the tags you do choose to insert are unobtrusive. For example, you can place the tag in the middle of a line ("What's happening?" Ron asked. "Did I miss something?"). Use this technique when there's a natural pause in the character's speech:

"Honey, I need to tell you something," Karen said. "Remember when you asked me not to spend any money this week?"

The best advice I can give you about dialogue tags is this: Try to strike a happy balance between using *said* after every speech and not using a tag at all.

Adverbs

Using excessive adverbs (descriptive words ending in -*ly*) in your dialogue is the mark of an amateur. Adverbs describe *how* something is done. By using an adverb in a dialogue tag, you *tell how* a character speaks instead of showing. Besides that, in many cases adverbs are redundant:

"John, are you awake?" Jane whispered *softly*.

Of course Jane whispered softly. How else could she whisper? No need to place that adverb in the dialogue tag. A writer can get away with this kind of thing once in awhile, but do it too often and you'll lose your audience.

Aside from annoying your readers, over-using adverbs indicates you're too lazy to write dialogue that speaks for itself. Compare these two examples:

"This soup is too salty," Fred said apologetically to the waitress.

"I'm sorry to bother you, but this soup is too salty." Frank slid his bowel toward the waitress without looking up. A glob of potatoes sloshed onto the counter and he dabbed it with his napkin. "Sorry about that."

The second example shows what Frank is doing and reveals something about his personality. This is much more effective than using the tongue-twister adverb "apologetically," although the better sentence took more effort to write. Most professional writers who use adverbs in dialogue apply them sparingly—perhaps one per page. For example, you may need to use an adverb to convey a character's words aren't being spoken as you'd expect:

"Well, aren't you cute," he said sarcastically.

"I still hate you," she said softly, running her fingers through his hair.

Better yet, avoid the adverbs and show the characters' state of mind through their actions:

"Well, aren't you cute." He threw down the newspaper and glared at her.

"I still hate you." She kissed his neck while running her fingers through his hair.

If you still can't resist the urge to combine adverbs and dialogue, consider the jokes called Tom Swifties, named after a series of boys' adventure books that used terrible adverb dialogue tags. These should help you get started:

"The temperature is dropping," he said coolly.

"I have a split personality," said Tom, being frank.

"Your fly is undone," was Tom's zippy rejoinder.

"I'll have a martini," Tom said dryly.

Present Participles

A present participle is a verb used as an adjective, and most often ends in *-ing*. These handy forms of speech function as adjectives and modify a pronoun or noun. For example:

opening (instead of open)

running (instead of run)

stopping (instead of stop)

chasing (instead of chased)

Using present participles in dialogue tags will help you define a character's actions, but some writers begin to rely on participles and use them too often.

Please note that *-ing* words cannot replace verbs in a sentence. "Running down the street to his house," is not a complete sentence. That's because the word *running* isn't a verb and the sentence has no subject. Which of the following are complete sentences?

1. Opening the cooler, he said, "I don't know about you, but I could use a drink."
2. Motioning for the waitress, "I don't know about you, but I could use a drink."
3. Stopping beside the water fountain, taking a huge drink.

The first example is a sentence, because it contains a subject (he) and a verb (use).

Numbers 2 and 3 are incomplete—no subject and no verb.

You get the idea. You'll notice famous authors sometimes misuse and over-use participles, but don't succumb to this temptation. It's a form of lazy writing, and here's why: Instead of using telling detail to describe an action scene, the writer tries to pack several events together.

- **Example:** Wrapping both hands around her neck, the man said, "Now I've got you!"

The above sentence should contain enough details for at least a paragraph, including the victim's reaction, the appearance of the man's hands, and the timbre of his voice.

- **Consider this sentence:** "Stepping off the curb, Frank slipped and fell under the wheels of a bus."

Yes, three things did happen to poor Frank, but not at the same moment. The writer omitted a couple of important steps. She took the lazy way out and ignored the details of his fall. What caused Frank to slip? Or was he pushed? Did he flail his arms and drop his briefcase?

- **Here's another example of incorrect use:** Planning every minute of the journey, Maria asked, "Why don't we stop at Niagara Falls for the night?"

The participle just doesn't work in that sentence. Perhaps it should read: Studying a map she'd found in the glove compartment, Maria asked, "Why don't we stop at Niagara Falls for the night?"

I'll say it again: Adding participles to dialogue helps show action and avoid adverbs as dialogue tags, but don't let them become a bad habit.

Adding participles to dialogue helps show action and avoid adverbs as dialogue tags, but don't let them become a bad habit. One per page is acceptable.

One per page is acceptable. Two is marginal. Three is excessive. If you've used more than two per page, you need to edit. And along the lines of "two wrongs don't make a right," please resist the temptation to tack adverbs onto a present participle:

- Whispering softly, Maria asked, "Why don't we stop at Niagara Falls for the night?

- Running quickly down the stairs, Joel shouted, "Wait for me, guys!"

- Breathing heavily, he chased Snoopy down the road, shouting, "Get back ere, you mangy cur!"

The adverbs do nothing to help this dialogue. If you do use present participles, let them stand alone.

EXERCISES:

1. Write a page of dialogue between two characters without using dialogue tags. Use gestures, actions, and props to help direct the reader.

2. Go over your scene and add a few dialogue tags to replace clumsy or overused gestures.

3. Rewrite the following scene without dialogue tags. Invent actions or props that show the characters' attitudes and tell us who's speaking.

"Harris, your sales figures hit rock bottom last month. What the heck's going on with you? Mr. Fisk asked.

Harris said, "I don't know, Boss. Guess I'm in a slump."

"I've noticed you're spending a lot of time with that new secretary in Accounting. I'd say you've lost interest in your work," Fisk said. "You used to be a real go-getter."

"There nothing to worry about, Mr. Fisk," Frank said. "I'll have my numbers up to par within two weeks. That's a promise."

4. Add a dialogue tag to the following sentence. Experiment by placing the tag in several different places to see how it changes the meaning.

"I admire your wife and think you're the luckiest man in the world, but I'd never try and take her from you. Not that she'd even let me."

5. Rewrite the following sentence three different ways without using the adverb (menacingly). Instead, follow the quote with a description of the speaker's actions or facial expression.

"You'd better get out of here," he said menacingly.

Chapter Six

Dynamic Elements

RESEARCHERS TELL US that 93 percent of communication is through body language, with the other 7 percent for words. During a conversation your characters may be eating, smoking, walking, having drinks at a local bar, or riding in a car. Background noises interrupt the flow of words as things happen around them: a cool breeze flutters the curtains, a car honks outside the window, a siren wails in the distance. Adding dramatic elements and telling detail to your dialogue will help readers form mental pictures—an internal movie—while they read.

Gestures

Gestures should reflect each character's personality and mood. Does the character sit calmly with her hands folded, or does she fidget with items on a table? Are her fingernails nibbled to the quick?

Don't use random actions—let each activity correspond to the personality traits you've established for that character. For example, a neatnik wouldn't shred his napkin and leave it scattered on the restaurant table. He'd stack the dirty dishes and place each used napkin atop the pile.

When my husband and I eat out, I flatten the wrapper to my straw and roll it up. Almost before the paper hits the tabletop, he snatches it up and adds it to the pile of used napkins he's accumulated on one corner of the table. He did this on our first date, and he's still doing it. Our personalities are opposite: I create clutter: He organizes. Where do your characters fit on the neatness spectrum?

As you develop characterization, think about the social gestures each person might perform. Picture your characters in different situations. An organized serial killer who meticulously plans each murder might use small, careful gestures. A killer smoldering with barely-suppressed rage would use larger, more aggressive gestures. What would each of these men do with a used match? Which of them would slosh coffee all over the table?

When adding gestures, don't use the first thing that pops into your head. Writers tend to over-use their favorite gestures.

Writers tend to overuse familiar gestures, so don't always go with the first thing that pops into your head. Tears trickling down a character's cheeks, narrowed eyes, raised eyebrows, twinkling eyes, and vision blurred by tears bring to mind an overwrought romance novel. Take time to refine each person's gestures until they fit the circumstances. In this example from *Up Island*, Anne Siddons skillfully weaves gestures and description into dialogue about a marital breakup:

He simply stared at me, then put his head into his hands. He laughed through his fingers, an exhausted, awful, little laugh.

"Molly, I may be a jerk and a cad and an asshole, but I am not a bigamist."

"You mean ... you mean you want to marry her, Tee?"

He lifted his head and looked at me with dead, red-rimmed eyes. "Jesus, what have I been saying to you for the past five hours?"

You might carry a notebook to record gestures and personal details that pop into your head during the day (but don't be creepy about it). Here's a sample from a lunch date:

- She fanned herself with the menu
- He winked at the waitress
- She grimaced
- He swirled a spoon in his coffee

The gestures you select should tell us about a character, help set the mood, and create a visual dimension to the conversation.

Symbolic Gestures

Perhaps you shudder at the mere thought of symbolism—having been browbeaten in a long ago literature class. I sympathize. But symbolism often creeps into our work without conscious thought, and you'll find it's a fantastic tool for enhancing and clarifying your story's theme. That's the macro view of symbolism.

On a micro level, you can weave symbolism into dialogue and character gestures, creating a rich tapestry of meaning.

On a micro level, you can weave symbolism into dialogue and character gestures, creating a rich tapestry of meaning.

Another passage from *Up Island* is a perfect example of the symbolic gesture. This describes the distressed heroine waiting in a doctor's exam room:

> I sat for a moment with my hands in my paper lap, one cupped on top of the other, a gesture like you make in Communion, waiting to receive the Host. I could not seem to focus my eyes. My ears rang.

Many writers use symbolic weather events—especially storms and dark clouds—almost as separate characters. In the opening paragraph of *White Oleander*, Janet Fitch lets wind and foliage set the tone for her novel:

> "The Santa Anas blew in hot from the desert, shriveling the last of the spring grass into whiskers of pale straw. Only the oleanders thrived, their delicate poisonous blooms, their dagger green leaves."

Symbols are powerful tools for a writer, but beware of overused cliché gestures, such as having a character pour a glass of water down the sink or take out the garbage after he dumps his girlfriend. A successful symbolic gesture rises above clichés to specifically describe the human condition.

Symbols are powerful tools for a writer, but beware of clichés.

Literary works are known for symbolism, especially *The Great Gatsby*. In this novel a green light stands for all Gatsby's longings and wants. When Nick speaks about the green light at the end of the book he says, "It eluded us then, but that's no matter—

tomorrow we will run faster, stretch our arms out farther..." In this way, Nick implies that everyone has a green light in the distance, just out of reach. Here's another example of symbolism:

> Waves foamed onto the beach, licking the edges of the castle we'd created. Soon the spires and turrets would be molded into a smooth lump of sand, then nothing. I turned to Alex. "We can't go on like this. Sooner or later, your wife will know."

The above symbol is heavy handed, but it presents the idea. The crumbling sandcastle represents the state of a relationship, or even the human condition. Consider these items as symbols:

- a feather floating in the wind
- the new moon
- an empty rocking chair
- a bird in a cage
- pebbles tossed into a pool

The most meaningful symbols in literature aren't contrived, but evolve naturally from the story—and that's where your subconscious mind comes into play. When seeking a symbol for your story, look to dreams and images that unexpectedly slip into your mind.

Consider your dreams a gold mine for symbols; keep a dream journal and interpret the images when you awaken each morning. Above all, don't force a symbol. If it's there, polish it. If not, write the story anyway.

Gestures as Character Tags

Connecting particular habits, gestures, and verbal tics to your characters helps readers more easily identify them. Perhaps a man lost his index finger in an accident and often massages the scar while he's speaking. Women sometimes brush hair back from their foreheads or touch their jewelry. A harried businessman might habitually glance at his watch.

Practice observing people for habits you can transfer to your characters. Watch a conversation from a distance and note body language, hand movements, and facial expressions.

Props

Here's an element to have fun with. Rarely are people alone in a scene without *something* physical, and these elements help move the story forward or reveal things about your characters. Props can include anything from a pitchfork to a tea cup. R. D. Wingfield, who writes the Jack Frost detective series, has a special gift for props:

> "You've got the cheek of the bloody devil," she snapped, banging three mugs on the table and hurling a tea-bag in each.
>
> Gilmore came in, shaking his head. "Wally wasn't in the house.
>
> "What did I tell you? I haven't seen him for days," smirked Belle, filling the mugs from the kettle and slopping in milk. "Help yourselves to sugar." She slid the mugs over.
>
> "So where is he, Belle?" said Frost, spooning out the dripping tea-bag and depositing it on the table.

Can you picture the surly expression on Belle's face as she serves the detectives? This paragraph would lose its spark without the tea, which gives Belle an opportunity to reveal her mood. Props and the gestures associated with them can fill a pause in conversation or define a silence. A lonely man waits at the bus stop, listening to snatches of conversation while he tosses breadcrumbs to the pigeons. A woman snaps open the bedroom curtains, flooding the room with light to get her lazy husband out of bed. Teenage boys discuss their girlfriends while they wax and polish a car. A drug dealer rolls a joint while speaking on the phone.

Cigarettes and smoking paraphernalia make convenient props, but they've become clichés. How many movies have you seen where people mix drinks or light cigarettes? Only write about these elements if you can present them in an original way, as R. D. Wingfield does with Inspector Frost:

1. Frost puffed out a smoke ring and watched it drift up and curl around the green-shaded light bulb.
2. A packet of Hamlet cigars lay on the dressing table. Frost shook it hopefully. It rattled. There was one left. He lit it, stretched out on the bed and contentedly puffed smoke across to the detective sergeant.
3. Frost lit up a cigarette and passed around the packet. Everyone took one, even Collier who didn't usually smoke. Frost looked down at the tarpaulin and prodded it with his foot. "I can't delay the treat any more." He nodded to Collier. "Let's have a look at him."

Notice Wingfield didn't add smoking to these scenes merely as a ploy to give characters something to do. In every case, smoking provides information about Frost's character or (in the final example) serves as a delaying tactic and covers the smell of a body.

Writers often use animals as props, especially for scenes where a character is alone. A cat who needs to be fed and watered, a dog, a tank of tropical fish—they give characters something to do at home. A pet may also reflect its owner's personality. Beware of animal clichés, and please don't make your characters have conversations with a goldfish, a cat, or any other non-human creature. Okay, maybe a few words here and there, but not a real conversation. Robert Dugoni introduces a bird to break up a long stretch of dialogue in *Damage Control*:

In the corner of the room, perched on a bar in his cage, stood Keeker, her mother's pink and white cockatoo. The bird squawked as they entered. Kathy picked up a package of sunflower seeds and pistachio nuts and filled the small plastic tray inside the cage to quiet him.

The conversation resumes after this brief interlude, but Keeker interrupts the scene several more times.

Have fun with props, using things you see every day and exotic items you'd like to write about. But before you add something to your dialogue, answer these questions:

- What does the prop reveal about the character?
- Does this prop advance the story?
- Does the prop reflect an element of the plot or tie into the story's theme?

Physical Contact

Don't overlook physical contact as you write dialogue. How people give and respond to touch reveals much about them. Have you ever been around someone who constantly invades your personal space—compulsive huggers, or women who feel compelled to pick lint from your jacket?

In the realm of touch, a gesture can signify many things. For example, a hand placed on the shoulder can impart reassurance, control, love, or a threat:

- With one hand on my shoulder, Pa guided me into the room. "Say to the teacher what you told me last night."
- She squeezed his hand, which lay across her shoulder. "Shall we move to the bedroom, Harry?"
- Freddy's hand was heavy on my shoulder and I felt the muzzle of his gun against my ribs. "Smile and act natural," he whispered.

Physical touch also works as a replacement for dialogue. When a mother kisses her daughter on the top of the head, she's saying, "I love you." A slap on the back from the coach means, "Go get 'em!" Lovers can make up after a fight by holding hands and smiling. Don't underestimate the power of touch to make the reader *feel* your character's relationships.

Don't underestimate the power of touch to help the reader feel your character's relationships.

Let's return to Robert Dugoni's scene with Keeker the bird:

> "I have cancer, Mom." Dana said the words as if they had been ripped from her body.
>
> "Oh, Dana." Kathy went around the table and pulled her daughter to her, holding her head against her chest, caressing her hair gently, as she had done when Dana was a child. Keeker continued to squawk and crack the shells in search of the soft seeds inside.

Here, a mother's touch is more effective than dialogue and the bird's actions add a nice symbolic touch.

Physical Sensations

Don't neglect the five senses in your dialogue: smell, taste, touch, sight, and sound.

As a character speaks, she may smell, hear, taste, and see what's going on around her. How she responds to physical sensations reflects her mental state and personality. John Sandford uses touch and smell in this passage from his novel *Chosen Prey*:

"Wonderful," he said, twinkling at her, the rope pressing in his hip pocket. She'd known the sex hadn't been that good—that's why she'd fled to the dishes. He bent forward, his hands at her waist, and kissed her on the neck. She smelled like yellow Dial soap. "Absolutely the best."

In *A Painted House*, John Grisham evokes images of country life:

The swing moved slowly back and forth, going nowhere, its rusty chains squeaking softly above us. Lightning popped across the road, somewhere on the Jeter property. "I had a dream about Ricky last night," she said.

When you develop your characters, consider what each of them likes and dislikes.

- Does someone have a phobia? Is your heroine addicted to Twinkies?
- "Don't you love the way this honey melts on your tongue?"
- "I adore the feel of fresh, white sheets."
- "Listen to that train in the distance. Don't it make you feel small?"
- "Pine needles smell like heaven to me."

Here's a tip about writing sensual details: Use active verbs and avoid the words "he saw, he smelled, he heard, he tasted." These words put distance between the character and the reader, because you're telling instead of showing.

When writing sensual details, avoid phrases that distance the reader from your character, such as "he saw, he smelled, he heard, he tasted."

Instead of being firmly inside a character's head and experiencing things as they happen to him, we see him from above. Often it's a sign of lazy writing and a way to avoid giving details. For example:

- He heard bells ringing in the distance. Better: Bells clanged from the south, far away.
- She saw Tom pull out a piece of paper. Better: Tom pulled a slip of paper from his pocket and frowned as he read it.
- He tasted the apple, then spit it out. Better: He spit out a half-chewed wad of sour apple.
- She smelled smoke from the kitchen. Better: A cloud of smoke drifted from the kitchen.

EXERCISES

1. Carry a notebook to record symbolic objects or interactions as you go through the day. Also note symbols from your dreams or daydreams. Save these notes to use in your writing.

2. Select a symbol and write a scene related to it. For example, a bird freed from its cage might relate to a girl leaving home for the first time. An empty rocking chair could symbolize the death of an infant or a woman unable to conceive.

3. Study people you encounter and take note of unique gestures or habits. Use these to broaden your characters.

4. Select a couple of props and decide how they might be used in a story. Write dialogue that includes the props. If you're stuck for ideas, try using a:
   - flashlight
   - rusty pocket knife
   - diamond necklace
   - toy gun

5. Draw a line down the center of a page. At the top of one column, write the word "Place," and for the other column

write "Props." Carry it with you for several days and take note of the props you find. Look for items that specifically relate to a place.

6. Write a dialogue scene that includes physical touch. For example, a woman who's been raped tries to tell her new boyfriend why she pulls away when he touches her. Don't forget to include sensory details.

Chapter Seven
Tension, Conflict, and Suspense

THESE THREE ELEMENTS are the heart of effective dialogue; the point where the dynamics of dialogue come together. If you don't build at least one of the three into every scene, you have no story. Dialogue without tension is flat and neutral, as exciting as a chat between two strangers in an elevator:

> "Nice weather we're having."
> "Yeah, but we could sure use more rain." "You work in the building?"
> "No, I'm here on business."

This conversation could drag on for several minutes before fizzling out from lack of tension. But what if one of the men began having chest pain and tried to hide his distress? What if one of them carried stolen diamonds in his attaché case?

Unlike conflict, which implies opposing views and opinions, tension is a dynamic element between two or more characters. Physical attraction creates powerful tension. In fact, sexual tension contributes to almost every best-selling fiction book on the market. For example:

> The humiliation of it was raw as the blood on her hands. "You son of a bitch."
>
> He shifted his grip to her knife hand, just in case. "I love you too, sweetheart. Now, I'll hang the bear. You go wash up."
>
> I shot it, I can—"
>
> "A woman who hesitates to listen to a man with a knife in his hand deserves what she gets." He smiled again, slow and easy. "Why don't we try to make this business go down smooth for both of us?"
>
> "It can't." All the passion and frustration that whirled inside her echoed in the two words. "You know it can't. How would you take it if you were standing where I am?"
>
> "I'm not," he said simply. "Go wash the blood off. We've got a ways to ride yet today."

The above passage from Nora Robert's novel *Montana Sky* sizzles with tension. Every encounter between these two characters heightens the suspense until the climax of the book, when they finally ... well, I won't spoil the ending.

In a different genre, Jim Mullen's book *It Takes a Village Idiot* features spirited dialogue between Jim and his wife. He creates tension throughout the book with conversations like this:

> "These people were nice enough to invite us out to the Hamptons, and this is how you say thank you?"
>
> "So I should shut up and act like a pod person?"
>
> "No one expects you to improve *that* much. You could just act like a normal person," Sue whispered.

The Mullens don't exactly argue, but there's always tension in their dialogue. External problems and props also add tension—another technique Jim Mullen has mastered:

> Sue has the kindling going and I drop the logs next to the wood stove. My beautiful, expensive trench coat is covered with moss, bark, dirt, dry rot, mushrooms, dead bugs, sap, seeds, and some round sticky burrs.
>
> "Two or three more loads like that should get us through the night," she says.
>
> "If not, we can always burn my coat. That should give off some heat."

Seasoned romance authors constantly throw their characters into situations that lead to conflict, and a character's personality traits usually help cause trouble. Curiosity, bravado, a quick temper, shyness, and almost any other tendency can lead to challenging situations and tension-filled dialogue. Willa, the heroine of *Montana Sky,* is stubborn and independent, refusing to compromise her ideas about how to run a ranch. When she's suddenly in charge of the place, her attitude creates conflicts with her sisters, the man she loves, and the men who work for her:

> "Goddamn women," Pickles muttered as soon as the door was safely closed behind her. "Don't know one that isn't a bossy bitch."
>
> "That's because you don't know enough women." Jim strolled over for his coat. "And that one *is* the boss."
>
> "For the time being."
>
> "She's the boss today." Jim shrugged into his coat, pulled out his gloves. "And today's what we've got."

Sometimes two characters' intense individualism pulls them apart, creating instant tension. Romance novelists play this to the hilt, but it works with any genre. On the other hand, characters who are too much alike will also clash. Combining difficult personalities and a challenging situation is a sure way to create tension for your dialogue.

Goals and Motivation = Tension

Analyze your own conversations and you'll realize almost every exchange has a goal. You're giving information, seeking information, or providing insights. Sometimes you're trying to reach a consensus or change someone's mind.

Analyze your own conversations and you'll realize almost every exchange has a goal. Along the same lines, people don't converse without motivation.

In other cases you're establishing rapport with someone or trying to get rid of them. Goals can be clear-cut or fuzzy, but your characters shouldn't engage in conversation without them.

Along the same lines, people don't converse without motivation. Motivation provides the reason behind a goal. Perhaps one of your characters is motivated by a desperate need for money. The goals of his conversation with the bank manager are to conceal a wretched credit history and obtain a quick loan.

Determine each character's motivation and goals before you write a scene; this will set the tension level for your dialogue. During any given scene your characters may be completely at odds with one another, partly disagree, or share a common objective that creates tension. For example, an interrogation scene between two police detectives and a suspect might contain the following goals and motivations:

First detective: His goal is to obtain information from the suspect and get a confession by any means necessary. He's partly motivated by frustration with his job and personal life.

Guilty suspect: His goal is to withhold information, protect his partner in crime, and convince the detectives he's innocent. He's motivated by fear of going to jail, possible retribution from his partner, and hatred for the cops.

Second detective: His goals are to obtain information from the suspect and prevent the first detective from using violence. He's motivated by disgust at the other officer's heavy handed tactics, plus a desire to protect the prisoner's rights so the case won't be thrown out of court.

Everyone's goals and motivations affect the dialogue. The two policemen are on the same team, but tension rises between them as they approach interrogation from different angles. Perhaps the first detective will come on strong while the second leans against the wall and adds an occasional question. Or the second man may take the lead to prevent the first detective from going ballistic. No matter how you work the scene, you've established tension that will lead to dynamic dialogue.

In the following example from *Night Frost*, R. D. Wingfield adds tension by having the Inspector Frost and his new partner disagree about policy. In this novel, Wingfield paired Frost with a rookie who isn't too bright.

> "We're wasting our time here," said Gilmore.
>
> "Maybe," said Frost, looking back at the house where a thin, bearded figure was watching them from the patio window. "But my philosophy in life is never to trust bastards with thin straggly beards."
>
> Burton started the engine as Frost slid into the passenger seat beside him.

"Back to the station, Inspector?"

"One more call, son. Let's check out the headmaster of Bell's school. I want to find out if there's been any complaints of Hairy-chin teaching advanced anatomy to the senior girls."

"We shouldn't be doing this," protested Gilmore from the back seat. "You're forgetting—Mr. Mullett said we should drop this case and concentrate on the stabbings."

"Mr. Mullett says lots of stupid things, son. The kindest thing to do is ignore him."

Notice how disagreement between the two policemen adds an element of tension to the dialogue; if the two officers agreed on what to do next, this passage would be less interesting. Throughout the book Frost is handicapped by his naïve partner, an incompetent superior officer (aptly named Mullett), and his own irascible personality.

Asking Too Much

Sometimes, in an effort to create tension, a writer packs too many elements into a single conversation.

Use these clues to detect dialogue that's trying to do too much:

- Do the characters restate things they already know?
- Are you presenting too much information?
- Does a character suddenly present new, disturbing information with no foreshadowing.
- Does tension come from an honest conflict between the characters or is it artificial, with no particular explanation?

If you've loaded a conversation with too many elements, you need to rethink the scene. Return to the basics. Determine each character's goals and motivations, and then revise the dialogue.

If you've loaded a conversation with too many elements, you need to rethink the scene. Return to the basics.

Perhaps you have a wife who's living in the past and a husband who wants to move on—literally and figuratively—by relocating to a new job. The wife makes excuses about why she doesn't want to move, but her real motivation is fear of leaving her family and familiar environment. Pretend you have no audience (the reader) and rewrite the dialogue. Don't worry about things the reader might not understand, such as the wife's close relationship with her mother. Add details later, and don't forget to read each passage aloud.

Internal monologues

Revealing a character's thoughts with internal monologues is another way to build tension and suspense. Like movies, books allow the reader to climb inside someone else's brain. If you've watched the movie *Stranger Than Fiction,* you'll know exactly what I mean. Every writer should see this movie, in which Harold Crick (Will Ferrell) hears an author (played by Emma Thompson) narrating his life. Imagine hearing this inside your head:

> **Voice of Karen 'Kay' Eiffel:** This is a story about a man named Harold Crick and his wristwatch. Harold Crick was a man of infinite numbers, endless calculations, and remarkably few words. And his wristwatch said even less. Every weekday, for twelve years, Harold would brush each of his thirty-two teeth seventy-six times. Thirty-eight times back and forth, thirty-eight times up and down. Every weekday, for twelve years, Harold would tie his tie in a single Windsor knot instead

of the double, thereby saving up to forty-three seconds. His wristwatch thought the single Windsor made his neck look fat, but said nothing.

And so it goes throughout the movie, until Harold finally meets the writer who had been living inside his brain.

Although writing an internal monologue is straightforward, beginning writers often have trouble with this technique. Instead of a glimpse into the character's inner life they present long-winded speeches and rambling thoughts. Each time you pause to delve into someone's mind, you're interrupting the story and short circuiting the action. First person lends itself well to internal monologue, but many writers fall in love with the main character's clever thoughts and forget about the plot. Resist the temptation to tell us everything your character is thinking. Preserve the mystery.

Science fiction author Hugh Howey has a masterful touch when showing a character's thoughts. In the clip below from *WOOL*, notice the questions Holston poses to himself. This is Howey's subtle way of guiding us to consider the right questions as the story continues:

> The view from the holding cell wasn't as blurry as it had been in the cafeteria, and Holston spent his final day in the silo puzzling over this. Could it be that the camera on that side was shielded against the toxic wind? Did each cleaner, condemned to death, put more care into preserving the view they'd enjoyed on their last day? Or was the extra effort a gift to the next cleaner, who would spend their final day in that same cell?

Creating these internal monologues is far better than having your characters think aloud. People do occasionally talk to themselves, but this doesn't work well in fiction. A character who goes around mumbling ends up sounding deranged.

Having characters speak to their pets is another tired plot device. If the pet is an obvious prop, readers won't buy into this technique.

"Well, Fuzzy, I wonder if I should call the police about that prowler we saw. Nah. They'd probably think I'm crazy."

Avoid using internal monologues to present backstory and information dumps. An information dump occurs when a writer inserts facts he believes we need to know into the story, oblivious to the fact that he's killing the suspense and short circuiting the plot. In the previous example, Hugh Howey presents vital information without being tedious.

The following example from a different author is a bit heavy-handed:

A year ago I'd be leading this team, Hank thought. He moved to the next tree, examined it for a moment to select his cutting place, and began swinging. Six other men from their village sliced at the trees. Two were his brothers, another his brother-in-law, two were cousins, and the youngest was a nephew. Just as he knew everyone in the village, he was related to most of them. Even the baron was a distant relation, a third cousin.

Notice how the writer wandered away from the story in his eagerness to present information about Hank's family—things we don't need to know at the moment. An internal monologue should have a direct bearing on what's happening in the story.

Understatement is the key to writing effective internal monologue. Do your best to avoid flowery prose and overblown emotions. Always remain true to your character's personality.

Passages written in thought mode should reflect each character's voice even more strongly than regular dialogue.

Understatement is the key to writing effective internal monologue. Do your best to avoid flowery prose and overblown emotions.

Inner dialogue can be a tension-building tool when we use it in moderation. Your readers should be dying to know what's going on in your character's mind. Only then, do you reveal his thoughts. Don't overdo it. When you run out of tension, conflict, or suspense, then move on to the next scene.

I can't resist closing this chapter with another wonderful quote from the screenplay *Stranger Than Fiction*. Imagine hearing this voice in your head:

Karen 'Kay' Eiffel: As Harold took a bite of Bavarian sugar cookie, he finally felt as if everything was going to be ok. Sometimes, when we lose ourselves in fear and despair, in routine and constancy, in hopelessness and tragedy, we can thank God for Bavarian sugar cookies. And, fortunately, when there aren't any cookies, we can still find reassurance in a familiar hand on our skin, or a kind and loving gesture, or subtle encouragement, or a loving embrace, or an offer of comfort, not to mention hospital gurneys and nose plugs, an uneaten Danish, soft-spoken secrets, and Fender Stratocasters, and maybe the occasional piece of fiction. And we must remember that all these things, the nuances, the anomalies, the subtleties, which we assume only accessorize our days, are effective for a much larger and nobler cause. They are here to save our lives. I know the idea seems strange, but I also know that it just so happens to be true. And, so it was, a wristwatch saved Harold Crick.

EXERCISES

1. Write a tension-filled dialogue between two people who've found something valuable and can't agree on what to do with it. One person wants to return the item, but the other wants to keep it. Before you begin, determine each character's motivation and goals.

2. Using one of your earlier dialogues, determine the motivation and goals of each character in the scene. Change the motivation and goals to see how that will alter your dialogue. Can you add more tension by changing a single character's motivation?

3. Using yourself as the character, invent an internal monologue revealing your thoughts and actions. Can you make it interesting?

Chapter Eight
Jump Start Your Story with Dialogue

HAVE YOU EVER THOUGHT of an amazing idea, spent hours developing it inside your head, and then watched the perfect scene float away when you couldn't decide how to begin?

Or perhaps you started a writing project and ran out of steam after the first few chapters. No experience is quite so humbling as staring at a blank sheet of paper or computer screen. Your resolve weakens. What seemed like an exciting adventure suddenly holds the appeal of a high school math assignment. You berate yourself. You delete files and start over. You find distractions, like killing flies or dusting the computer screen. Maybe you even give up.

Do not despair! Setbacks are part of the writing process. You aren't solving equations—you're tapping into your creative mind, which can be temperamental and elusive.

I've learned to use dialogue when I need a quick way to jumpstart a writing project—either fiction or nonfiction. You might begin writing dialogue with a specific plot in mind, or you can start with a random sentence and see where it leads. Your first efforts at this will resemble a script, but don't worry. As the plot evolves you can move the dialogue further along in the story and open it with narrative. But for now, let dialogue help you survive the dreaded opening scene jitters.

Opening with dialogue is called beginning a story *in media res*—in the middle of things—without using narrative to set the scene and give background information. Challenging? Yes, because your readers have no context for the dialogue, so why should they care? Most editors and agents don't like to see a book start this way. As I mentioned above, you can begin with dialogue at first, then change your mind later and add a scene before your characters begin speaking.

In *The Last Coyote,* author Michael Connolly successfully opens his book with dialogue. We don't even know who's speaking at first:

> "Any thoughts that you'd like to start with?"
> "Thoughts on what?"
> "Well, on anything. On the incident."
> "On the incident? Yes, I have some thoughts."
> She waited but he didn't continue. He had decided on the way to Chinatown that this would be the way he would be. He'd make her pull every single word out of him.

Anyone who reads Connolly's novels knows this is typical behavior for Detective Harry Bosch, a character loved by millions of fans. How does one find a magic opening line?

Listen to the people around you. Almost any dialogue you overhear could begin a story.

Let's take the words, "Please help me!"

In Chapter Six, I randomly attached those words to a woman struggling with a bag of groceries. It might also apply to a swimmer who's drowning, a child who can't tie her shoelaces, or an elderly person lost on the street. Close your eyes and let your imagination carry you into a scene. Think of one line.

Write your sentence on a piece of paper, or complete a list of possible situations below it:

"Please help me!"

1. An old woman is walking in the street. She wandered away from her house and doesn't know where she is.
2. A five-year-old child struggles to tie his shoelaces, but can't get it right. He approaches his older brother, who's busy playing.
3. A woman in the grocery store can't find her young child.
4. A woman struggles with a bag of groceries and her abusive partner refuses to help.

Each of your ideas could spark an entire scene with several characters. To keep things going, have another character answer the first line you've written. Remember, the dialogue should contain tension, so don't resolve the problem right away. Here are possible responses to the above situations:

1. "Please help me!" (old woman) "Get out of the way." (a man passing by)
2. "Please help me!" (little girl) "Have Mom tie your shoe laces. I'm busy."(brother)
3. "Please help me!" (frustrated shopper) "Sorry, I'm on break." (irritable clerk)
4. "Please help me!" (woman carrying groceries) "What is it now?" (her boyfriend)

Select one of the scenes you've written and begin adding details. Who are these people? Where are they? How did they get into this situation? Can you develop a story from two lines of dialogue?

Here's how I began a story about the woman carrying groceries: I imagined an Englishman named Rollie, well educated, but violent;

a con man and drifter who recently hooked up with Sandy, the daughter of a rich businessman. Sandy lives on the third floor of a tenement, and she's a drug addict. Her father funded numerous treatment attempts, but finally gave up. Now he mails Sandy a check once a month and tries to forget about her. Rollie is already tired of her.

Using the sentences of dialogue you've written, follow my example and create at least two characters. Begin writing notes about their relationship. Remember, if these people aren't having serious problems, you have no story.

Set the Scene

After visualizing Rollie and Sandy in my mind, I create Sandy's apartment—a hot, dirty tenement crawling with fleas from the dogs her ex-boyfriend owned. Dirty dishes overflow the sink and cockroaches scurry out of sight when the lights come on. Sandy has blotches all over her body; she's sick.

Sandy tripped on the stairs and swore under her breath, nearly losing her grip on the brown paper sack he'd given her. The plastic bag dangling from her wrist banged against the banister. Her breath came in huge gasps.

"Please help me!"

"What now?" Rollie glared at her from the top step.

"I'm about to lose these bags, you creep. I need help."

He kept walking, but shouted over his shoulder, "Leave the heavy bag on the steps and go back for it." After setting his own bag on the landing, Rollie unlocked the apartment and kicked the door open, wincing at the sour odor of garbage.

Which character carries the point of view? I can't tell yet, but I need to make a decision so readers will know who's telling the story. Usually the best point of view character is the one with the most to lose. I might construct the scene two ways and see which I like better.

This is where I ran out of ideas. I could visualize the apartment, but I didn't know what to include or leave out. So I decided to continue writing dialogue and fill in the details later. I wrote an entire page of dialogue in present tense with only a few descriptions, like a screenplay. Here's how it worked:

Crimey, it's like a blessed oven in here." Rollie turns on the fan. "What's wrong with you, anyway? You've got red spots all over."

"It's flea bites. The damn fleas are eating me alive. I need a hit." Sandy pulls out a crack pipe.

Rollie grabs the pipe and throws it. "Just look at yourself. You need to lay off for a couple of days."

"Mind your own business." Sandy grabs the pipe and retreats to the bedroom. "Suit yourself. It's your life." Rollie sits and thinks. He considers leaving.

He hears her vomiting in the bedroom and decides to investigate. He takes a washcloth in to her.

"Here. Wipe your ugly face."

I could turn this vignette into a story or save it to use later. Now it's your turn. Continue writing a scene for your characters. Focus on dialogue, and then sketch in the action and settings as they occur to you.

What's the Problem?

In the above story, Rollie and Sandy are fighting over her drug use. What problems do your characters face? What are their motivations and goals? Put yourself inside their minds and imagine how they respond to pressure. .

Now add details to your dialogue so the reader can picture the characters as you see them. Here's how I carried on with the scene between Rollie and Sandy:

Crimey, it's like a blessed oven in here." Rollie switched on the fan above the kitchen table and sat below it with his feet propped on a chair. "What's wrong with you, anyway? You've got red spots all over?"

"It's flea bites. The damn fleas are eating me alive."

She was right. Her last boyfriend had kept three pit bull terriers in the apartment, and they left behind a legion of hungry fleas. The bugs didn't bother Rollie, but they'd bitten Sandy all over. She scratched constantly, like a hound with mange.

"I need a hit." Sandy perched on the edge of a straight backed wooden chair and rummaged through her purse. She produced a bag of white powder, a cigarette lighter, and the thin plastic tube she used as a crack pipe. When she looked up at him, a thin stream of blood trickled from her right nostril.

"You stupid cow!" Rollie grabbed the pipe and threw it across the room. "Just look at yourself. You need to lay off it for a couple of days."

"Mind your own business." Throwing him an evil look, Sandy snatched the pipe off the floor, grabbed her purse, and retreated to the bedroom

"Suit yourself. It's your life." Rollie opened the kitchen window and settled at the table with a cold beer. Sandy was a huge disappointment. She'd been nothing like he expected. Six days ago he'd fallen under the spell of her honey blonde hair, pale blue eyes, and shy smile. How could he know she was a crack head? Sex was a waste of time, because all she thought about was her next hit. He stayed around because the apartment was one step above sleeping in his car, and because she told him her dad sent a fat check on the first of every month. An hour ago she'd cashed the check and spent most of it on drugs. With great effort he'd convinced her to invest in a twelve pack of beer and some canned food.

He popped open a beer and considered his options. At this point he'd just as soon kill her. But he had nowhere to dump a body, and the apartment smelled bad enough without adding to the stench.

Vomiting sounds came from the bedroom. He switched on the radio to drown out the noise, but after a few minutes curiosity got the better of him. He wet a washcloth under the bathroom tap and carried it in to her.

"Here. Wipe your face." He tossed the cloth at her. She lay half naked on the sagging mattress. Light filtering through the curtains gave her face a green cast.

Now I've fleshed out the story, although I still don't know where it's going. Later I'll worry about the outcome, but this is a good start. Now, do the same thing with your story.

A Turn for the Worse

Once I set the scene for these characters, I wanted to make things worse for them. By then I'd decided to use the encounter between Rollie and Sandy as the opening of a science fiction story about a deadly virus. Here's how it continued:

Sandy groaned and pressed the washcloth to her face. "I feel like crap."

Rollie gagged and held his breath to keep from smelling the vomit. The room reeked of something horrible, and blood trickled from her nose. "You're in bad shape. I'd better call someone." He threw a towel over the mess she'd made.

"I'll be all right. Just bring me a beer."

When he came back a few minutes later, Sandy was making gurgling sounds with each breath and the skin around her mouth looked gray. She couldn't hold the beer can, but he pressed it against her mouth so she could drink. She sputtered, trying to swallow and breathe at the same time, then fell back onto the pillows.

He left her alone for an hour, thinking she might sleep it off. When he checked again, she was barely breathing and ugly bruises had formed on her arms and thighs. The skin on her forehead was cold and clammy.

Rollie pocketed the money from her purse, stuffed his belongings into a suitcase and walked out, leaving the door ajar. He stopped at a pay phone inside the corner grocery to call 911, but changed his mind and dropped the coins back into his pocket. Let Daddy handle this one.

Now that you've written a beginning for your characters, can you develop an unexpected development that adds to the tension or suspense of your story? Continue writing your scene and let it develop until you reach a temporary resolution.

The Jump Start Technique

Use this method when you reach an impasse in your writing or need to find ideas for a new project.

1. Write one line of dialogue.
2. List several situations your dialogue might fit.
3. Choose the most intriguing situation and write an answer to the first line of dialogue.

4. Continue the exchange between these unknown characters until you can see them in your mind's eye.

5. Develop their personalities a bit further. Who are these people? How did they get into their present situation? What are their motivations and goals?

6. Now, picture the scene using all five senses. Add sensory details.

7. Write more dialogue, filling in the characters' actions as though you're writing a screenplay.

8. Go over the scene several times, adding more details with each pass. Focus on dialogue, but sketch in the action and setting as they occur to you.

9. Consider the problems your characters face. Can you make things worse? Add any unexpected developments that occur to you.

10. When you edit this scene you may need to remove unnecessary dialogue. For now, leave it alone and keep writing.

Chapter Nine
Children's Dialogue

CHILDREN'S BOOKS ARE NOT AS simple as they seem. The short, delightful story you just read to your child was probably written by a savvy author who eliminated thousands of words to reach the core of her tale.

You can find dozens of books about writing for children and they're crammed with helpful advice for writers. You probably know this market is complex, crowded, and difficult to break into. If you're serious about writing for children, mastering the art of dialogue will boost your credibility as an author.

You probably know this market is complex, crowded, and difficult to break into. If you're serious about writing for children, mastering the art of dialogue will boost your credibility as an author.

Years ago, children's stories contained mostly description and focused on moralistic tales, told in stiff, proper language. Today's children won't tolerate this kind of writing—they're accustomed to television, texting, interactive games, and instant feedback. But even the most sophisticated children respond to a good story well told, which explains the ongoing popularity of fairy tales and other books that keep selling year after year, such as the *Little Women* series, *Little House on the Prairie*, and *Anne of Green Gables*. The authors of these books tapped into universal themes and used vivid dialogue. Here's a selection from one of Laura Ingalls Wilder's book:

> "When the fiddle had stopped singing Laura called out softly, "What are days of auld lang syne, Pa?"
>
> "They are the days of a long time ago, Laura," Pa said. "Go to sleep, now."
>
> But Laura lay awake a little while, listening to Pa's fiddle softly playing and to the lonely sound of the wind in the Big Woods, She was glad that the cozy house, and Pa and Ma and the firelight and the music, were now. They could not be forgotten, she thought, because now is now. It can never be a long time ago."

These tips will help you master dialogue for children's stories:

Choose your target age group. Feel free to experiment, but when you're serious about writing for children, focus on a specific age. Don't attempt to write for all ages at once. Research children's developmental stages and apply this to your writing. What do these children study in school? What social skills are they developing? What are their relationships with siblings and parents?

Are the children in your audience capable of reading by themselves, or will they have your stories read to them? Spend time with children of this age and ask questions. Notice their conversations.

Will you write fiction or nonfiction? Naturally, fiction will contain dialogue, but nonfiction also benefits from conversations sprinkled into your writing. However, beware of making up dialogue you *think* a historical character would have spoken. Fabricated dialogue makes the story fiction. Instead of making it up, look for published interviews where you can find punchy quotations or dialogue with an interviewer. Let your subjects speak for themselves whenever possible and don't forget to source every statement they make in your references section.

Think like a child. Try writing an incident from your point of view, then rewrite the scene from a child's viewpoint. Whatever you do, don't talk down to your audience or use baby talk. Respect their intelligence by using rich, interesting language that evokes strong visual images, but avoid the temptation to treat children like miniature adults.

Read books and stories for young people. Find out what books are popular and read them. Ask yourself why young people enjoy the books. How does the dialogue differ from adult books? Study classic children's books, such as *Black Beauty*, and read the winners of the Children's Book of the Year Awards, the Caldecott Medal, and other prizes. And I beg you—please don't write another *Harry Potter* clone.

Read stories written by children. Many web sites provide stories and ezines featuring children's own writings. This is a great way to learn how children view the world and how they express themselves. For example, Stone Soup is an online magazine featuring young writers and artists at www.stonesoup.com.

Share your stories with children. Read your stories aloud to children and watch for reactions. Ask questions to see if they understand what you're saying and how they feel about the characters. Ask if the characters and dialogue seem real to them. You'll get honest opinions from this audience.

Listen to children's conversations. How do they speak? What do they talk about? Remember, you're writing *for* children not *about* them. If possible, record and transcribe a conversation.

Avoid trendy slang. Cartoon characters, current events, and the latest action figures come and go within a few weeks—and so will your book if you include these items. Often, by the time you finish your manuscript, a new trend will be all over the media. Using slang will date your work before you even find a publisher.

Join or start a writers' group to focus on writing for children. Networking with other writers will inspire you, especially when they give feedback and critique your work. You can also find websites for children's writers.

Visit libraries and talk with the librarians about what children like. Study available books, especially the titles everyone wants to check out. Attend library programs for kids, such as read aloud sessions, or arts and crafts

Visit playgrounds, shopping malls, and other public places. Watch children interact with one another and with adults. Imagine how you'd act and feel if you were one of the children. Carry a notebook and jot down ideas for stories. Warning: Men should be careful about this activity. In this day and age, a man who watches children may appear suspicious.

Make sure your characters don't all sound the same. Focus on differences in speech and mannerisms. How do girls differ from boys in the language they use and their gestures?

What about cultural influences? In some cultures, girls are much more restrained than boys.

Don't avoid conflict and problems. You may want to write happy stories, but without conflict, suspense, or tension you have no plot. Children deal with stress and problems every day, and sugarcoating the world doesn't help them deal with it.

Children deal with stress and problems every day, and sugarcoating the world doesn't help them deal with it. Young people find reassurance when they see a character overcome challenges.

Young people find reassurance when they see a character overcome challenges. For young children the problem may be simple, like surviving the first day of school or losing a tooth. Older children face complex situations, such as divorce and death. Either way, you should encourage thinking and never preach moral messages: Be subtle. As successful children's writer Mo Willems says, "Always think of your audience, but never think *for* your audience. What that means is to leave it open to interpretation. I'm not telling things, I'm asking questions. And I'm asking questions that I don't necessarily have the answers to."

The Christmas Spurs by Bill Wallace tells of a boy whose younger brother dies from leukemia. It's a story of sadness, love, and hope. Here, Nick's brother, Jimmy, has just undergone medical tests:

> "What's wrong with Jimmy?" I demanded.
>
> Mama reached out and hugged me tight against her. I thought she was crying because of the way her tummy jerked, only I couldn't see any tears. "Nothing," she managed.
>
> Daddy came in about then. He was all dusty and grungy from mowing the dirt (there wasn't much grass to mow). I turned to him. "What's wrong with Jimmy?"
>
> He ruffled my hair and looked at Mama. "Nothing."
>
> Something was wrong. Bad wrong. And since nobody would tell me what, I was going to find out for myself.

The Christmas Spurs is about real children who confront a problem they don't understand. By the end of the book, the author answers their questions. If your goal is to make children feel better about themselves, then show your characters interacting with the real world and triumphing, not living in a safe fantasy world.

Make 'em Laugh. Children love to laugh, so don't forget to include humor in your writing. But do your homework by studying what amuses children. Young children enjoy lively dialogue that constantly moves the story forward. Dr. Seuss' books are timeless examples. Use vivid, descriptive words. A single word can make a sentence funny, or dull. Here's a review for *The Unruly Queen* by E.S. Redmond:

> E.S. Redmond, where have you been all my life? How did you come up with the most marvelous first page of a children's book that I may have ever read?

> "Minerva von Vyle was a mischievous child
> who was coddled and spoiled and allowed to run wild.
> She was peevish and pushy and got her own way
> by throwing hysterical fits every day."

> Minerva is a slightly older and darker Eloise but, luckily for Minerva, she is about to meet a nanny who knows just how to handle her. With gorgeous illustrations and a wickedly funny story in verse, this has jumped to the top of my favorite books list. As a testament to its perfection, my four-year-old son has already memorized his favorite pages and it's in heavy rotation during bedtime. Minerva would be pleased.

Suspense is crucial, and we know children love it. Long-winded descriptions of background information or scenery will never hold their attention, so read your work aloud to identify boring passages and long-winded dialogue. Use lots of white space (action plus dialogue) to keep things moving.

Rethink those talking animals! Talking animal tales went out of vogue several years ago, but now they're back in style. However, it's vital to develop a unique personality and dialogue style for each animal—exactly as though it's a human character. Everything your animals say should reflect their personalities. Don't fall back on stereotypes like dirty pigs, industrious hens, and flighty grasshoppers. Surprise yourself and your readers.

Avoid expository dialogue. Dialogue must be more than narrative surrounded by quotation marks. If your dialogue consistently has characters explaining their actions to the reader, then it's flat and boring. Here's a brief example of expository dialogue:

> Jill whispered to Fluffy, her stuffed bear, "I don't know where my mother went. I'll search the house and see if she's hiding somewhere. Maybe she's in the basement. I'll look down there."

This author could produce a better story by using narrative passages to show details:

Holding Fluffy's ragged arm, Chris hung over the stairwell and called, "Mom, I'm ready for breakfast. Where are you?" No one answered. The house felt quiet, like no one else was home. Where did Mom go? Maybe she was doing laundry in the basement.

Avoid pedantic dialogue. Smuggling vocabulary words into your dialogue is usually a bad idea, because when you work too hard at trying to teach something the message overwhelms the plot. We've all been forced to read these stories in school, and they aren't something we choose on our own. Here's an alternative:

Humor and exaggeration make effective teaching tools. If you want to expose children to new words, provide a bookworm character who reads the dictionary for fun and tries to fit new words into everyday speech, with disastrous results. Or develop a funny character who garbles big words. How about a spelling-bee contestant whose mother makes her memorize five new words every day?

Think multicultural. Publishers are looking for stories featuring children in specific world cultures.

Publishers are looking for stories featuring children in specific world cultures.

However, beware of focusing on a culture you don't know, because publishers also want authenticity. Authors writing about a culture other than their own often make errors of fact and omission.

No matter when you were born, you experienced a particular culture with unique characteristics. The best stories are based on personal experience or folktales heard in childhood. A recent article in *Book Links* stated:

> The increase in multicultural books has resulted in a wide range of folktales, some historical novels, and a good number of nonfiction books about African Americans, Asians, Latinos, and native Americans... Yet there are still far too few high-quality novels and picture books featuring children of these cultures (especially native American and Latinos) as protagonists in contemporary settings.

You'll find many opinions and controversies about who should write these books. Some people believe authentic books can only be written by a member of an ethnic group who's immersed in its cultural traditions. Other critics say authors can write authentic books if they have experience and awareness of other cultures and are willing to do painstaking research. One thing is certain: if you aren't familiar with a culture, you should never write about it off the top of your head. That's especially true for dialogue.

Avoid stereotypes, don't oversimplify or romanticize a lifestyle, and make sure you understand the role of females, elders, and family within the culture.

Don't be hung up on pop culture. Writing about passing trends is a sure way to date your book, and that includes slang and trendy words in your dialogue. Yes, kids often speak in code; they use broken sentences, invent their own languages, and interrupt one another. No problem—you can show this with dialogue. Use contractions and keep the action going, but don't fill the story with this month's popular words or references to current rock stars and movies. Instead, focus on your basic message. Here's a refreshing word on the subject from children's author Mo Willems:

> I'm very lucky to write for children, because I don't have to deal with popular culture. I can just deal with core fundamental issues: jealousy, love, hatred, sadness, joy, wanting to drive a bus. The fundamental core emotional things. And just asking questions like, 'How do you know when you're in control? What is a friend? What are relationships between people?' These are all things that I haven't figured out yet. I'm very lucky in that I don't understand the world yet. If I understood the world, it would be harder for me to write these books.

A Child's Viewpoint in Adult books

Child narrators can live in your readers' hearts long after the story is finished and the book is back on the shelf (a real shelf or a virtual shelf). However, it takes a magic touch to make child characters interesting to adults and still keep the naive viewpoint. No one wants to read two hundred pages of a real five-year-old's life.

Beyond that, you need a firm grasp of your narrator's characteristics—including age, temperament, and manner of speaking. Your character may be precocious, but don't let him slip out of character and suddenly start acting or speaking like an adult.

Child narrators can be wonderful, because they bring a fresh, innocent viewpoint to your story. They question things we take for granted. Looking through their eyes, we see the world in a new way. You can explore family situations and even social issues without becoming preaching or having an obvious agenda, as Harper Lee did with racism in *To Kill a Mockingbird*.

While your child narrator probably won't use adult vocabulary, she can still be articulate, inventive, strong, and passionate—and she can say things an adult narrator couldn't get away with. You'll find excellent examples of dialogue from a child's point of view in these books:

A Painted House by John Grisham
The Yearling by Marjorie Keenan Rawlings
To Kill a Mockingbird by Harper Lee
Hearts in Atlantis by Stephen King
The Education of Little Tree by Forrest Carter

Here's a sample of dialogue from Harper Lee's classic novel *To Kill a Mockingbird*:

"Hey."
"Hey yourself," Jem said pleasantly.
"I'm Charles Baker Harris," he said. "I can read. You got anything needs readin' I can do it."
"How old are you," asked Jem, "four-and-a-half?"
"Goin' on seven."
"Shoot no wonder, then," said Jem, jerking his thumb at me.

"Scout yonder's been readin' ever since she was born, and she ain't even started to school yet. You look right puny for goin' on seven."

"I'm little but I'm old," he said.

Notice Lee doesn't write cute dialogue. In fact, the children's speech is confrontational as they size one another up. The conversation sounds real, enhanced by that undercurrent of tension. Children's dialogue needs this tension and it should move the plot forward as though they were adults.

Lee's novel follows three years in the life of eight-year old Scout Finch, her brother, and their father, Atticus—a time punctuated by the arrest and eventual trial of a young black man accused of raping a white woman. Writing as a child allows Lee to address racism and prejudice through innocent eyes.

Many other authors have used this technique, including recent books by Stephen King and John Grisham. Grisham's seven-year-old narrator takes us to rural Arkansas in 1952. He witnesses a series of events that range from the dramatic to the profoundly disturbing—including a birth, a flood, and two killings.

When writing in first person from a child's viewpoint, develop vivid internal dialogue that reveals your narrator's inner life:

> I would pick cotton, tearing the fluffy bolls from the stalks at a steady pace, stuffing them into the heavy sack, afraid to look down the row and be reminded of how endless it was, afraid to slow down because someone would notice. (*A Painted House*, by John Grisham).

You should know your main character inside and out—her dreams and fears, her favorite things, how she feels about her family, and how she reacts when things go wrong.

You should know your main character inside and out—her dreams and fears, her favorite things, how she feels about her family, and how she reacts when things go wrong.

Create a character profile, listing everything from favorite color to favorite article of clothing. Make a list of her favorite words and expressions, what she's currently learning in school, and how her speech is molded by her culture. Of course you can use your own childhood as a reference. The following suggestions will help you prepare to write from a child's viewpoint:

1. Study children from the age group of your narrator. Listen to speech patterns, especially when they're under stress.

2. How do children in this age group interact with adults? Your hero or heroine should be old enough to carry on a conversation with adults and to understand most, but not all, of the situations he encounters.

3. Read essays and stories written by children in the age group of your narrator to help you understand how your character thinks and views the world.

4. Do some reading in child psychology to determine what developmental tasks your character needs to achieve. For example, the developmental tasks of adolescence include adjusting to a new physical sense of self, developing a personal sense of identity, and establishing emotional and psychological independence from parents. Understanding and developing each character's psychology will help you grasp his point of view and produce better dialogue.

5. How does your character address adults and authority figures? Does he show respect? Is he flippant?

6. Collect pictures that remind you of your characters.

7. Close your eyes and recall a vivid childhood experience, using all your senses and including dialogue. Write a scene describing the experience from a child's viewpoint.

Chapter Ten
Mastering the Screenplay

AH, THE ALLURE OF HOLLYWOOD! What writer hasn't fantasized about publishing a bestselling book and then writing the screenplay for a blockbuster movie? Stephen King and John Grisham are prime examples of novelists who moved on to Hollywood. In 1989, Grisham published his first novel, *A Time to Kill*. The book received a few reviews and moderate sales. However, his next book, *The Firm*, was a break-out hit. In 1990, before the novel was published, Paramount Pictures secured the film rights for $600,000. Now, almost anything Grisham writes hits the best seller list and has potential to become a successful movie.

Even more exciting, consider science fiction author Hugh Howey, a self-published writer who clawed his way onto the New York Times bestseller list and is now working with a producer on the movie version of *WOOL*, his post-apocalyptic tale about people who live belowground because the outside world is toxic. Casting begins in 2014 and people are saying this movie will be a blockbuster when released in 2015.

This could be YOU. Let's delve further into the relationship between books and movies.

Book–or Screenplay?

Novelists sometimes wonder whether they should adapt their project into a screenplay, perhaps even before the novel finds a publisher. Screenplay writers wonder if their project should be turned into a book. Skip Press, author of the *Writer's Guide to Hollywood Producers, Directors and Screenwriters' Agents*, advises writers to create a book first and then the screenplay.

Experts advise writers to create a book first, and then the screenplay. Chances for publication are greater for a book.

Press contends the chances for publication are greater with a book than a screenplay, and if the book is published and then sold to Hollywood, the writer will make more money on the deal.

Adapting a novel into a screenplay may appear simple, but it's a completely different process than writing a book. Before you even begin the screenplay, ask yourself:

- Does my story fit any of Hollywood's genre niches?
- Is the story dramatic and visual enough to become a movie?
- Could the characters be cast with box office stars?
- Is the story line unusual, but still within a typical established genre?
- Could the film be produced for a reasonable price?

Before making the jump into screenwriting, study the genre and learn basic skills. Here are five tips from the experts:

1. Learn the standard formatting for screenplays and follow it. Don't deviate. Purchase at least one book on the topic, such as *How Not to Write a Screenplay* by Denny Martin Flinn. Attend workshops and take classes if possible.

2. Less is more, as with all writing. Avoid creating large blocks of action. The total page count should be 90 to 120 pages.

3. Don't write anything that can't be filmed. Your dialogue and actions should reveal what characters are thinking—don't tell us.

4. Always read your script aloud multiple times, with other people reading the parts.

5. Even the best dialogue can't overcome a weak plot. Create a strong story supported by sparkling dialogue.

The movie *Good Will Hunting* is known for spirited dialogue and the natural-sounding repartee among Will and his buddies. The writers achieved this realism by speaking the dialogue before writing it. You can practice this technique by having someone improvise a scene with you. Always read your dialogue aloud, preferably with another person who'll take some of the parts. Make an audio tape and listen for flaws. Do the conversations sound natural?

Dialogue should "sound good" on the page. The person who evaluates your script won't have the luxury of hearing it read aloud. She'll have to grasp the characters' state of mind from the words, phrasing, and punctuation you select. If you aren't familiar with screenwriting techniques, buy a few books on the topic and study published screenplays.

Do you think professionals have it easy? In an interview titled "The Hardest Scene to Write," Spike Jonze discusses a scene in the critically acclaimed movie *HER.*

...there's one scene about two thirds of the way into the movie, where they're sitting on a roof and Samantha says, "I'm writing a piece of music, and Theodore asks her what the piece of music is about. I must have changed the answer completely about five times—and even within those five ideas, there were so many different versions, so we must have redone that scene about twelve different times.

Here's how the resulting dialogue appears in the screenplay:

EXT. PARK – DAY

Theodore sits on a bench in a park on a rooftop wedged between tall buildings. There's not really any view besides the trees in the immediate foreground. People sunbathe and exercise. He sits, eating a sandwich, his device next to him. He looks at the device, then out at what she's looking at.

THEODORE

What are you doing?

SAMANTHA

I'm just sitting here, looking at the world and writing a new piece of music.

He looks at the world with her for a minute.

THEODORE

Can I hear it?

She starts playing it for him. We hear this beautiful, romantic piece of music.

Tricks of the Trade

Create a specific vocabulary and manner of speech for each character, and reveal this in the character's first speech. Speech tags, such as "y'all" and "yep" can be useful tools.

Some characters will use complex sentences, while others favor short, disjointed sentences.

Don't forget to include broken phrases in your dialogue.

Creating a code of speech for groups of characters helps identify them and show bonding. People who work together in an office use common phrases. Medical professionals use specific slang words, as do guys who hunt together, firemen, and people who share almost any profession or sport. Do your homework and learn these words, because they make the audience feel like part of the group.

Maintain suspense by having your characters interact like bumper cars or dominos. Each encounter should provoke a reaction of some kind, and your characters should discover new things about themselves and each other.

Use silence. Sometimes it reveals more than words.

Use miscommunication. This is a powerful way to add tension and suspense to your story, but it must be believable. Nothing is more irritating than a character who withholds important information for vague reasons. (Don't you hate those romance novels where the hero and heroine won't say "I love you" because of some weird hang-up that doesn't make sense?)

When you write an action scene, keep in mind what your character's body is doing. Don't expect an actor to make a long speech while running from the police. Get rid of questions that require only a short answer. Instead, use open-ended questions that expose more about your character.

MARILYN

How was your day?

JOHN

Rotten, since you ask.

The previous exchange takes up space without revealing anything about the characters. An open-ended question produces more information:

MARILYN

Something tells me you a bad day.
What happened?

JOHN

Well, I was late to work because the damn alarm
clock broke, and then I spilled coffee on my shirt
right before the big meeting. Naturally I had to
introduce somebody, and I looked like a total
idiot. You wanna hear more?

Accents and dialect

At some point you'll need to write dialogue for a character who has a foreign accent or speaks a dialect. Changing the spelling of words to communicate an accent makes the dialogue hard to read and confuses the actors. Simply state that your character has an accent, then reinforce this through sentence structure and word choice. In *The Green Mile*, Frank Darabont indicates southern accents through his choice of words and the rhythms of speech:

COFFEY

Boss?

Needs ta see you down here, boss.

PAUL

Got things to tend to just now, John Coffey.
You be still in your cell now, y'hear?

For another character, Darabont does change the spelling of a few words to indicate a Cajun accent:

DEL

What dat man do to you? He throw some gris-gris on you? You look diff'int! Even walk diff'int! Like y'all better.

Dialogue should speak for itself

If you feel the need to punch up your dialogue by underlining specific words or giving stage directions, it's a dead giveaway the dialogue isn't good enough. In well-constructed dialogue, actors instinctively know which words need emphasis and how to react as they speak. Here's an example of bad screenwriting:

HANK

Hey, I'm <u>really</u> sorry about last night. I should've been here sooner.

He looks up at her.

MOLLY

Stop apologizing, Hank. The worst is over and we're all <u>fine</u>.

She smiles at him.

HANK

But I <u>do</u> owe you an apology.

Interpreting every line of dialogue with stage directions for the actors slows the reading and destroys the scene's rhythm. Likewise, underlining words will drive the actors crazy. Don't include acting notes in your script unless they're unavoidable.

If you find yourself needing to explain everything you write, you'd best rewrite the dialogue. Instead of providing directions, put your character in a situation during which, based on his personality and the storyline, he could only feel one way

Common dialogue flaws

Wooden dialogue comes across as stilted and formal when read aloud. A character's speech should seem natural and reflect his personality, background, and circumstances.

Also consider the attitude behind the words. Here's a well-written passage from *The Green Mile*, adapted by Paul Darabont:

PAUL

I'll chew that food when I have to. Right
now I wanna hear about the new inmate
... aside from how big he is, okay?

BRUTAL (smiles)

Monstrous big. Damn.

DEAN

Seems meek enough. Retarded, you figure?

PAUL

Looks like they sent us an imbecile to execute.

HARRY

Imbecile or not, he deserves to fry
for what he done. Here...

> Harry tosses a pair of manila envelopes
> bound with rubber bands on the desk
> before Paul—Coffey's file.

The previous passage sounds authentic and provides information about the new prisoner and the guards' attitudes. The writer uses slang and incomplete sentences to make his dialogue flow like real speech.

Predictable dialogue lacks tension and suspense. If the audience can always tell what's coming next, why watch the movie? Reread your script and look for predictable conversations. Find ways to show more about your characters and surprise the listener.

Use other means of expression, such as physical gestures, to help avoid a trite exchange of words. For example, if a character says, "I love you," instead of replying with the expected "I love you too," her husband might say something funny—a secret joke between them.

Disjointed dialogue leaves the reader scratching his head. Writers who aren't accustomed to screenwriting sometimes forget what the reader does and doesn't know. Keep track of what you've already written and avoid letting your characters go off on tangents. Characters should listen to each other and respond accordingly. Also, don't throw too much information into a single scene, especially the opening act. Readers will only remember about three points from each scene.

Don't throw too much information into a single scene, especially the opening act. Readers will only remember about three points from each scene.

Slang has the same shelf life as a loaf of bread, so don't let it date your material. Invest in a slang dictionary and select words and phrases that won't be out of style before your screenplay is produced.

Get rid of dialogue that narrates the action. If people are shown something on the screen, then don't have your characters say it. If we see Marilyn's horse cross the finish line, there's no need for her to shout, "My horse won the race!" Just show her jumping up and down, ticket in hand. Also avoid having your characters state the obvious. If they're huddled together under an umbrella, no one has to say, "It's raining."

Avoid dialogue that focuses on one subject for too long and slows the story. If you've written more than two or three pages of dialogue to address a single issue, you're in danger of losing the script reader or movie viewer. If you must continue the dialogue, cut to a different scene and then return to find the characters still talking.

Avoid long monologues. An unbroken speech that runs more than a page can alienate your audience. Of course, there are exceptions to this rule, such as courtroom dramas where the attorney makes a closing summation. But notice that while the attorney speaks the camera doesn't always stay with him; it pans the jury, the judge, the audience, and the defendant.

The same goes for a minister who's delivering a long sermon. As he rants and raves, we notice reactions from the congregation. Some of them may be asleep, others gaze out the window. Only a few grandmothers fan themselves with the program and listen attentively. The general rule is: keep one speech to three lines or three inches.

The first draft

Remember, the first draft of your screenplay is supposed to be bad. Just get your character's voices on paper and worry about the rewrite later. Sometimes it helps to write scenes out of order.

Focus on the scene you hear and see most clearly, and then write the next one. Before long, you'll have a complete screenplay ready for editing.

EXERCISES

1. Tape a television show you enjoy and analyze one scene at a time. What was the scene's tone, or mood? How did dialogue reveal the character's personalities? What didn't you like? Write your own scene with the characters from the show.

2. Write the dialogue for the following scene: A woman tells her boyfriend she's dating someone from the office. Have her reveal this information in an unexpected way.

3. Obtain a screenplay and read it, then watch the movie and follow along with the screenplay. Analyze what you like and dislike about the movie, with emphasis on dialogue. Was the dialogue believable? Were the characters interesting and well developed?

4. As you study a written screenplay, note how the writer used dialogue and action together. Write a dialogue that includes action. You might use two police officers in their car deciding whether to pull over a suspicious looking vehicle or follow it.

5. Write a scene that includes more than two people interacting. Choose characters who come from different social and economic backgrounds. You might use a car filled with senior citizens on their way to a funeral who've just collided with an old, uninsured van driven by a Hispanic man who speaks little English. The van is carrying several illegal immigrants. You take it from there.

Chapter Eleven

Dialogue in Creative Nonfiction:
Journalism, Family History,
Journaling, Poetry, and Memoir

Journalism

PROFESSIONAL JOURNALISTS UNDERSTAND the power
of dialogue and new reporters are often told, "Use a good quote
high in the story." Quotes in a news story or personal interest piece:

- bring a human touch to the story.
- show much about the person who's speaking—often things
  the journalist couldn't say by herself.
- help frame the issue being discussed.
- introduce a topic and give a preview of what's to come.

Many journalists have bolstered their careers with juicy quotes
from sports heroes, music icons, and film stars. Celebrities aren't
the brightest people on the planet, but for some reason people
want to know what they think. However, can you guess the problem
with quotes? They often represent talking heads. In most cases, we

have no idea where the speaker is standing or sitting. Tossing in a quote also interrupts the action, which can be distracting.

And that brings us back to dialogue. Quotes give information, while dialogue enriches a story. You can include dialogue from an interview or discussion. You may overhear heated dialogue, such as an angry exchange at the local school board meeting or from demonstrators out front. Sometimes dialogue is implied, as in this high school sports story:

> Allen worked for nice post position and was fed the ball. The junior center made a nice move and knifed in to scoop it in for points 1,000 and 1,001 early in the third quarter.
>
> A teammate made it official.
>
> "When it went in and everybody kind of screamed up in the crowd, Dom came over and whispered, 'Welcome to the club.' That told me I'd definitely made it and it was a good feeling."

Family History

Rich data bases on Internet sites like FamilySearch.org, Ancestry.com, and RootsWeb.com have created an addictive new hobby for millions of people: genealogy and family history. The Internet now offers more than dates and names: family history sites are rich with documents such as diary pages, land deeds, newspaper articles, photographs, and more.

Sometimes people want to write about their families in vivid detail, using the language of the times and imagined dialogue. This is a hybrid genre known as creative nonfiction—containing hard facts and historical data, but using the literary devices of fiction (voice, character development, and dialogue).

Your first step is to develop a sense of the voice your characters will use. Perhaps you'll find diary entries or the memories of family members to help with this task. If you're interviewing people about the family, ask if they remember favorite sayings, speech patterns, and conversations. If someone's telling a story, ask if she can repeat the actual conversation. You may hear things such as this:

- "Mother always used to tell me... "
- "I remember the time Grandpa talked to us about his days in the coal mine. He said..."
- "I sure do remember what the teacher said to me after I picked a fight with Tom..."

My grandmother told me stories about things her grandmother said to her—unfair rules that still rankled after seventy years. You can turn memories like this into scenes with dialogue. Since you'll be speculating about many things, it's a good idea to keep the dialogue simple, but you can still create an effective dramatic scene. For example, my grandmother recalled having to sit in the loft of their log cabin with her strict grandmother while a party with fiddle music and dancing went on downstairs. She wasn't allowed to join the fun, and at the age of 92 she still remembered the pain of it all—and could repeat the words of Uncle Billy when he begged to take her downstairs for just one dance. This would be an easy scene to write and it's important for our family, because my great-great-grandmother's straight laced attitude shaped how my mother and her sister were raised, which in turn influenced my upbringing.

As an example of family history, I recommend you read *The Deeds of My Fathers* by Paul David Pope. In this fascinating tale of the men who created *The National Enquirer*, Pope relied on more than 500 interviews, using this information to forge dialogue that reflects what was *probably* said. For example, the following dialogue describes his young grandfather speaking with an agent for a shipping company that offers passage to America:

"How much is the fare for America?" Generoso asked.
"Ten dollars."

"How old do you have to be?"

"Sixteen."

"I can't wait."

"Look here." [Generoso shows the agent a letter from his brother-in-law in NY offering to sponsor him when he arrives in America.].

"Would you like to see some pictures of New York?"

"Oh, yes! Very much."

Even though Pope didn't know the exact words spoken at this meeting, he made an educated guess based on his family research. This dialogue brings the scene to life without taking any great leaps of imagination. If you use this kind of dialogue, ponder what each person was thinking and feeling. Research speech patterns for the time and place, along with historical details. If you keep within the bounds of historical accuracy, you can use dialogue to entertain readers and tell an intriguing story.

Journaling

Your life story is unfolding every day, and who could tell it better than you?

Your life story is unfolding every day, and who could tell it better than you?

Dialogue is one of the easiest ways to enhance a personal journal with colorful, vibrant events. Dialogue adds excitement to written journals and also scrapbook journals, where you can create a display of photos, drawings, and meaningful objects to surround a conversation. One simple, yet effective approach is to document each side of a conversation, as in a screenplay. Here's a sample from an online article by Myra Cherchio:

Me: (casually) So, you have a girlfriend? Really?

Jake: (being cool) Yes.

Me: How do you know she's your girlfriend? Does she hold your hand?

Jake: No! Mommmmmm!

Me: Well, how do you know she's your girlfriend?

Jake: Because she's in LOVE with me.

In a scrapbook journal, this conversation might be accompanied by a photo of Jake, and other memorabilia. This is *your* journal, so don't hesitate to add thoughts and feelings about the conversation. You may decide to thread your thoughts between lines of dialogue, which can help eliminate dialogue tags. In the following sample from Debbie Hodge, notice how she packs everything into a single paragraph:

Jake walked into the room during a show that I knew wasn't age appropriate. It was about child abduction. He immediately latched onto the content and started launching questions in true Jacob style. "Mom, what would happen if someone took me? What would you do?" Sensing a parent moment, I tried my best to stay in control. "Jake, if something ever happened to you, my heart would be broken in a million pieces. There's nothing I wouldn't do to find you." But Jake wasn't stopping today. His little mind was already in full swing. "Mom, if you lost me, wouldn't you just lay another kid?" When I looked puzzled, he went on. "You know mom, make one come out of your tummy." It took a second to register. Lay. Egg. Chick. Hatch... Kid??? "Jake, I could never replace you with another kid." That would never happen. I only ever wanted you. You're the only Jacob for me." To which he replied, "I don't know mom. There are a ton of Jacobs in my school." Ok, now this is getting hard. Too fast. "But Jake—there is only ONE Jacob

Anthony Cherchio in the whole wide world. I am quite certain of that."

Disaster averted. Jake's concern seemed to be abated (and The Talk Delayed)—for the moment. But that little mind is always ticking. Always thinking. Always hatching another question for a new day.

You'll also want to include precious one-liners in your journal—things you hear from family members, friends, and even people you don't know.

You'll also want to include precious one-liners in your journal—things you hear from family members, friends, and even people you don't know.

Record comments that bring back memories, make you smile, or even make you cry. A single, intriguing line of dialogue might preface a larger topic you want to explore:

- "I need to tell you, I've been seeing someone else." (Who couldn't follow this with several angst-ridden pages of journaling?)
- Husband to me: "Honey, you're snoring." (The first time you're forced to acknowledge this un-ladylike habit)
- "Excuse me, Ma'am" (Ma'am? Am I really that old?)

If a friend says something hurtful, write it down, along with your feelings. A situation at work can be analyzed in the journal with dialogue:

It was agonizing, but we finally pulled the plug on Cody, our assistant manager. When I told Cody he was fired, he looked bewildered and said, "But I've been trying really hard the past two weeks."

"Yes," I said, "But you knew we were watching you because of the stuff you pulled earlier."

He shrugged. "I never liked this job anyway. You guys really suck." Three second pause. "Will you give me a good reference?"

As an author, you may wish to keep a separate journal to record ideas and work out internal problems during a project. One of my favorite writing books is John Steinbeck's *Journal of a Novel: The East of Eden Letters,* written by Steinbeck as he composed the novel *East of Eden.* He composed the letters (journal) on the left-hand pages of a notebook, while using the facing pages for test writing *East of Eden.* He used this exercise to cleanse his mind of daily trivia, express doubts and worries about the book, and prepare himself for writing. He might follow a passage about his characters or choice of pencil (pencils were a big deal to Steinbeck) with details about building a new desk or buying items for the house. But thoughts of the novel always return, "waiting and working is kind of like a fermenting mash out of which whiskey will be made eventually." "Now," he signs off on March 16, "it is time for me to go to work."

Steinbeck found a good use for his writer's journal. I suggest you forget about rules when you're journaling. Don't think twice about cramming an entire conversation into one paragraph, neglecting punctuation marks, and leaving out dialogue tags. The journal is your place to be creative. Integrate photos, colored paper, stickers, drawing, and other motifs into the pages, so you can tell a moving story.

Memoir

A memoir is a collection of memories *from* a life, while an autobiography is more factual in nature—the story *of* a life. The beauty of memoir comes from a writer's ability to transform ordinary events into scenes that tap into a deeper truth. At one time, no one dared write a memoir unless he or she was famous, terribly rich, or titled. The rest of us were boring. But over the past ten years, everyday people have been captivating readers with personal stories. Your memoir might be a personal journey for yourself, your close friends, and family. Even so, you may choose to turn it into a book with limited distribution.

For example, our friend Bruce Hronek of Indiana University has a distinguished career in forestry and law. He conducts seminars nationally and internationally on legal liability, philanthropy, recreation, and natural resource management. He authored or co-authored three textbooks for universities. But, for me, Bruce's best book is the memoir he published for family and friends, titled *A Full and Exciting Life*. He only had fifty copies of this book printed and you won't find it for sale, but his words are a treasure to those of us who know and love him. As Bruce explains his work:

> I hope this abridged history will help future generations learn about their heritage and understand that, although we may be years apart in age and our time on this earth may not coincide, all who share the human family must overcome adversity and find excitement and joy in life's journey, regardless of where it takes them.

A memoir needs to be interesting if you expect anyone to read it. Unlike journaling, you're writing for an audience, not just yourself.

A memoir needs to be interesting if you want anyone to read it. Unlike journaling, you're writing for an audience, not just yourself.

Therefore, forget about including every detail and explaining each event. Always consider your readers.

Try and discover themes in your life. Every memorable artistic work contains a universal theme, and this is especially important for memoir. A theme is a universal idea anyone can understand. For example, the themes in Bruce Hronek's memoir were family and spiritual growth. You may discover such themes as courage, conflict, and sacrifice. Instead of telling a group of stories that aren't connected to one another, why not create a work of nonfiction that leads your readers' hearts to a deeper truth?

A memoir should be personal, not a collection of sterile facts and events. Focusing on intimate details will help your readers connect to the story.

A memoir should be personal, not a collection of sterile facts and events. Focusing on intimate details will help your readers connect to the story.

Where were you and what were you doing when your husband proposed? Describe the scene and how you felt. Even better, add dialogue. Don't be afraid to expose yourself, even the ugly parts of your story. Your mistakes, your angry words, the people you hurt— these things become part of who you are. The best memoirs dig deep instead of skimming the surface. If you want your story to matter, you must show your humanity.

You may choose to focus on a single time period in your life, as Gin Getz does in her memoir *The Color of the Wild: An Intimate Look at Life in an Untamed Land*. This book follows Gin and her family during one year in the wilderness, but she also writes about her early life and connects everything to her theme: Learning to bend and grow within the trust of shared isolation. And Gin isn't afraid to expose her weaknesses:

Like most everything I do, I learned the hard way about solo horse packing. You know. Start first. Learn along the way. And hope for the best. Fortunately, the best thing I learned is that it's not so hard. The biggest obstacle is, of course, fear.

And where does dialogue come into a memoir, you might ask? You already know by now that dialogue will make your story more interesting, real, and readable. You probably know it's impossible to remember the details of conversations from years ago, or even last week. The trick is to maintain each character's voice and use dialogue to reveal character, keep the story moving, and add texture to the scenes.

Don't record every word of a conversation; only use the best parts—the words that reveal emotional truth. For an emotionally charged scene, you probably remember one of two lines that were spoken, and that is all you need to begin re-creating an entire conversation.

Here's a dialogue excerpt from *The Daily Coyote*, a memoir by Shreve Stockton. Shreve is discussing her recent estrangement from Charlie the coyote. Notice how much better this is than a narrative and how it reveals her raw feelings:

"It feels like a lifetime ago, that we were like that," I said, heartbroken.

"It's probably just hormones, with mating season right around the corner," Mike said. "Think of him as a cowboy sittin' in a bar at two in the morning, and he can't find a woman so he just wants to fight. That's all it is. It'll be okay."

I didn't totally believe him but couldn't help but burst out laughing.

If you keep a journal, write a family history, or create a memoir that includes dialogue, you'll be leaving a vital legacy for your family.

If you keep a journal, write a family history, or create a memoir that includes dialogue, you'll be leaving a vital legacy for your family.

Other Nonfiction

Almost any nonfiction book will be more attractive to readers if you add dialogue, quotes, and interviews. The spoken word is compelling, extra white space looks good on the pages, and dialogue will increase your credibility. Here's an example of dialogue in *Confessions of a Community College Administrator* by Matthew Reed:

> An exchange at home with my (then) six-year old daughter:
> "Daddy, what did you do at work today?"
> "Well, I had a bunch of meetings."
> "But what did you *do?*"
> A few months later she invited me to "career day" at her school, to try to explain to her first grade class just what it is that I do all day. The best I could come up with was, "I try and get grown-ups to play nice and share their toys." They looked puzzled, and I quickly turned it over to my friend the chemical engineer, who explained molecules by dancing among the chairs.

Reed's wit and the lively, informal writing style save this book from becoming another boring academic memoir. I enjoyed learning what a college administrator faces every day.

Dialogue is also important for how-to and self-help books, where authors should include interviews with experts in the field, along with sample conversations, when appropriate. In *I Do, Part 2* (a book about life after divorce), author Karen Buscemi enhances her book with an abundance of stories from people who've "been there, done that." The quotes Buscemi uses always support the points she's making.

My friend Leslie started dating before her first divorce was finalized. She ended up in a four-and-a-half-year relationship, which included her new man and his kids moving into her home two years into the relationship.

"It was really one big happy family," she says of her time with this suitor. "My son loved it." When the relationship ended, Leslie helped her son get through it by encouraging him to stay in touch with the kids. "He's still friends with one of the kids today."

However, Leslie says after her second divorce she changed the way she dated and involved suitors in her kids' lives.

"I'm way more private now," she says. "I'm way more picky about when I introduce someone to my sons."

Self-help authors often employ sample conversations to show what might be said by the reader or someone else. In their book *Slow Parenting Teens*, parenting experts Molly Wingate and Marti Woodward make the book more useful by including sample conversations where parents and teens interact in fast parenting versus slow parenting. Each chapter of the book opens with a quote from a parent or teenager, such as:

"I don't argue with my mom because she always listens. That doesn't mean I get my way, but we just don't fight."

—Hannah, fourteen years old.

"I learned to stop trying to mold my daughter into a different person and accept her as she is."

—Martha L., Colorado Springs

"Even though my son is only twelve, I learned that communicating my fears to him now is important."

—Nancy D., Colorado Springs.

Author and communication professor Ellen Bremen goes one step further in her book *Say This, Not That to Your Professor*. She uses "What You Might Say" and "What Your Professor Thinks" at the beginning of each chapter:

What You Might Say: Everybody's confused about that writing assignment

What Your Professor Thinks: Telling me how other students feel doesn't help you.

What You Might Say: Joe got a 92 and I only got an 88, but we have the same check marks on our score sheet.

What Your Professor Thinks: Asking why you didn't get what Joe got is the fast track to misery for both of us.

Throughout her book, Bremen adds credibility and interest by including dialogue between herself and students, sample conversations between students and professors, and catchy headings, such as:

Ask Yourself This:

Think This:

Not That:

Say This:

Not That:

What You Have the Right to Say:

Of Course You Wouldn't Say:

You can see how Bremen uses dialogue and why her book is a huge success with college students and professors. The author's advice is not only right on target and timely—her book is also easy to read and entertaining. If you're a nonfiction author, you can't go wrong by adding the human voice to your writing, through dialogue, quotes, and sample conversations.

Dialogue Poetry

Did you know there are over fifty types of poetry, ranging from sonnets to limericks? Dialogue poetry has been around for a long time and was favored by William Shakespeare. Basically a dialogue poem is a conversation between two characters that may give voice to opposing viewpoints or illustrate a theme.

Concrete imagery and vivid descriptions are vital to poetry, along with choosing exactly the right words. In a poem, each word is a building block. Picture yourself constructing a wall with fieldstones of different shapes and sizes. Each stone must fit beside the others, bear weight, and help support the wall. And so it is with the words of a poem.

Many poets like to write on the computer where they can move words around on the page, seeking the ideal arrangement. The poems you end up with may be serious and deep, or lighthearted and quirky. Here's a classic example of dialogue poetry from Raymond Carver, whose literary career was devoted to short stories and poetry:

Plus
by Raymond Carver

"Lately I've been eating a lot of pork.
Plus I eat too many eggs and things,"
this guy said to me in the doc's office.
"I pour on the salt. I drink twenty cups
Of coffee every day. I smoke.
I'm having trouble with my breathing."
Then he lowered his eyes.
"Plus, I don't always clear off the table
when I'm through eating. I forget.
I just get up; and walk away.
Goobye until the next time, brother.
Mister, what do you think is happening to me?"
He was describing my own symptoms to a T.
I said, "What do you think is happening?
You're losing your marbles. An then
you're going to die. Or vice versa.
What about sweets? Are you partial
to cinnamon rolls and ice cream?"
"Plus, I crave all that," he said.
By this time we were at a place called Friendly's.
We looked at menus and went on talking.
Dinner music played from a radio
in the kitchen. It was our song, see.
It was our table.

Here's another Carver poem. In this one he uses direct speech to add dramatic effect:

Gravy
by Raymond Carver

Gravy.
Gravy, these past ten years.
Alive, sober, working, loving, and
being loved by a good woman. Eleven years
ago he was told he had six months to live
at the rate he was going. And he was going
nowhere but down. So he changed his ways
somehow. He quit drinking! And the rest?
After that it was all gravy, every minute
of it, up to and including when he was told about,
well, some things that were breaking down and
building up inside his head. "Don't weep for me,"
he said to his friends. "I'm a lucky man.
I've had ten years longer than I or anyone
expected. Pure Gravy. And don't forget it."

Are you ready to try this? Starting with a theme in mind is one way to begin your dialogue poems, although I find it's easier when I'm inspired by a single line of dialogue I hear someone speak, or certain words stick with me and touch something inside. A theme is always hidden somewhere within these words.

Starting with a theme in mind is one way to begin your dialogue poems, although I find it's easier when I'm inspired by a single line of dialogue.

Of course you need to know your characters and make them distinct. Less is more in poetry, so you won't be providing background stories, but it's still crucial for you to know these things. Edit your poems to the bare bones, leaving only words that must be said and do not distract from the message. With poetry, simplicity is always best, and your conversations can be unconventional.

Only start editing after you've put everything you want to say on paper. Don't turn off that creative flow until you're finished. The more material you have to work with, the easier it is to find your story. Finally, read the poem aloud, and then ask someone to read it to you.

Here's the beauty and the fun of poetry: You may choose to ignore those tiresome rules for punctuation and grammar. Dialogue poems have no right or wrong form; you can pretend your poem is a snippet from a story; you can make it rhyme, or not rhyme; you may forget about dialogue tags or use them; and feel free to include as many characters as you want. Your only obligation is to make sure readers get the message.

EXERCISES:

1. Read a newspaper looking for quotes and dialogue. How well do they work? Try using dialogue and quotes in the next piece you write.

2. Try something new in your journal. Add dialogue, plus creative images such as photos, drawings, or other designs. If you don't have a journal, it's time to start one! If you're stuck you can find dozens of web sites and books with journaling prompts and other ideas.

3. If you're a serious author, start a journal for your writing. Use it to warm up for a writing session, practice writing dialogue and other elements of a story, and to preserve ideas, such as overhead conversations.

4. Pick a theme for your memoir. What will it be about? Forgiveness? Redemption? Spiritual growth?

5. Begin writing your memoir with one scene that sticks in your mind. Or start with today. What's going on in your life right now? Write about the present, and then segue into related memories.

6. Read memoirs by other writers and notice how they use themes, dialogue, description, and other elements.

Memoirs You May Enjoy

Angela's Ashes by Frank McCourt

Eat, Pray, Love by Elizabeth Gilbert

Night by Elie Wieasel

Out of Africa by Isak Dineson (also known as Karen Blixen)

The Glass Castle by Jeanette Walls

The Year of Magical Thinking by Joan Didion

This Boy's Life: A Memoir by Tobias Wolff

Tuesdays With Morrie by Mitch Albom

Chapter Twelve
Dialogue in Graphic Novels

AS A KID WHO GREW UP loving comic books, I have no gripes with this genre. Comics are definitely lightweight reading, but calling them *graphic novels* makes this genre seem more artistic and sophisticated. As author Daniel Raebum wrote,

> I snicker at the *neologism* first for its insecure pretension—the literary equivalent of calling a garbage man a 'sanitation engineer'—and second because a 'graphic novel' is in fact the very thing it is ashamed to admit: a comic book, rather than a comic pamphlet or comic magazine

Writer Neil Gaiman, responding to a claim that he does not write comic books but graphic novels, said the commenter "meant it as a compliment, I suppose. But all of a sudden I felt like someone who'd been informed that she wasn't actually a hooker; that in fact she was a lady of the evening."

However you define a graphic novel, our mission here is to explore writing dialogue for this exciting genre. Even if you're doing it just for fun, creating a graphic story is a perfect way to practice writing pithy dialogue.

Even if you're doing it just for fun, creating a graphic story is a perfect way to practice writing pithy dialogue.

For this genre, you must keep it short, because overblown dialogue ruins the graphics. Do you want your characters to lurk behind giant speech balloons crammed with words? Of course not. Instead, you strive for balance between images and words. You may use captions from time to time, but don't rely on them to carry the story. Dialogue is much more powerful.

You will need plenty of action and excitement in your story. Pictures of people standing around talking do not show action. Graphic characters shouldn't be introspective for more than one frame. People in graphic novels do not ponder, mull, and discuss: They act.

Pictures of people talking do not show action. Your characters will not be introspective. Graphic characters shouldn't be introspective for more than one frame. People in graphic novels do not ponder, mull, and discuss: They act.

The average demographic for graphic novels is between ages 16 and 35, which includes a huge variety of fans. You needn't write about super heroes and dark villains; the story can be a love tale, a spiritual lesson, a historical book, a biography—almost anything you choose.

Formatting the Graphic Novel

Here's the good news: You can write the script for a graphic novel without drawing the story. An artist will take care of that. The length for a graphic novel is usually 88 to 132 pages, and it may be self-contained or a continuing story. Count on about six panels per page in your graphic book, with one visual concept per panel.

The layout for a graphic is much like writing a script, but more detailed. And, you'll use text boxes. Along with the dialogue, you will add actions and even sound effects for each panel on the page. Each panel has a number, plus action describing what happens inside the panel and dialogue for the characters to speak. You'll find an excellent tutorial at this Web address: http://2012.scriptfrenzy. org/howtovformatcomicbooks and http://2012.scriptfrenzy.org/ introtocomicbooks

Page 10

PANEL

1. Harried looking writer sits at desk in front of old computer. Desk is cluttered with cups, pens, and other junk. A thick manuscript is piled beside him. KLACK – KLACK – KLACK GOES THE KEYBOARD. Joe flings his arms up.

2. JOE

I can't believe it! My novel is done! After ten years!

3. The door behind him opens. Standing there is Betty, a look of disbelief on her face.

BETTY

We need to celebrate. Let's go out tonight.

You'll be able to use four to six panels on a single page, usually with only two characters per panel. On average, two script pages should equal one graphic book page, but there's no rule for this. If you want to use a caption from a narrator, a passage from a diary, or a voice inside someone's head, create a "transition" box and write those words inside it.

You'll need to create a synopsis that covers the entire plot, along with a description of each character—including general appearance. This will help you keep track of the story.

No problem having panels without dialogue where the action speaks for itself. However, in the script you'll need to describe that action and the characters' facial expressions. The artist does need direction, but don't get carried away with details. The action may include sound effects. (Splat! Crash!) Directions for a typical action scene might read:

Joe and Betty step into a taxi, dressed for a night on the town.

If you still think graphic novels are old fashioned and silly, check out this review from Booklist for the first book in the SAGA series by author Brian Vaughan and illustrator Fiona Staples:

Vaughan, writer of the hugely successful *Y: The Last Man*, isn't one to think small. In this opener to his ambitious new series, bits of sf space opera and classic fantasy mesh in setting a sprawling stage for an intensely personal story of two lovers, cleverly narrated by their newborn daughter... Vaughan's whip-snap dialogue is as smart, cutting, and well-timed as ever, and his characters are both familiar enough to acclimate easily to and deep enough to stay interested in as their relationships bend, break, and mend. While Vaughan will be the star power that attracts readers, do-it-all artist Staples is going to be the one who really wows them. Her character designs dish out some of the best aliens around, the immersive world-crafting is lushly detailed and deeply thought through, and the spacious layouts keep the focus squarely on the personal element, despite the chaotic cosmos they inhabit. Add another winner to Vaughan's stable of consistently epic, fresh, and endearing stories.

—Ian Chipman, Booklist

This is high praise for a mere comic book. Here's a brief sample of that "whip snap dialogue" the reviewer likes:

Alana: *Why are you crying? You never cry. What's wrong, Marlo? What is it...*
Marlo: *It's a girl. She's perfect.*
Alana: *Look, she's gonna have your horns.*
Marlo: *And your wings.*
Alana: *But what's with those eyes?*

While this isn't exactly Shakespeare, it's excellent dialogue for a graphic novel, and SAGA tells a compelling story. Plus, the artwork is incredible. Now it's your turn to write a graphic story:

EXERCISES

1. Read graphic novels of all types until you have a strong feel for the genre. What type of book do you want to write?
2. Print a few pages of a graphic novel you like and blank out the text, including the bubbles. Re-write the dialogue using your own words. Then redesign the characters, giving them different personalities. Write that dialogue. How many different ways can you interpret the visuals?
3. Outline a story you'd like to use for a graphic novel. Then fill in the blanks and create a synopsis. Write an overview of each character.

Chapter Thirteen

Editing Dialogue:
The Finishing Touches

AS HE WATCHED ME WRITING a rejection note to an author, my husband inquired, "What makes a good book?"

I thought for a few minutes, and then reported back to him: "I love to start reading and completely forget about the writer. I don't notice him behind the scenes, manipulating the story or the dialogue—everything flows together, like it was meant to be."

Achieving this kind of writing requires skill, talent, perseverance, and something else in the end: the ability to edit your work. Editing will make your work more accurate, vivid, and compelling. We edit for several reasons:

- because we sometimes fail to notice familiar problems. Every writer falls into the habit of writing a certain way. Sometimes we don't recognize our flaws until we look a second and third time.

- because we want to perfect and publish our work. If your rejections slips say, "It just didn't grab me," then you need to edit.

- because we care about our readers and know they deserve the best.

Editing dialogue requires no special skill or magic potions. Following a checklist will simplify the process. Feel free to use all or part of the following tips:

Read Aloud

Reading your work aloud is one of the best ways to improve your writing. Here's why:

- Your breathing pattern will tell you when sentences or speeches are unnaturally long.
- You may find you've started three conversations in a row using the same words.
- You'll notice the sound of words as your read. Eliminate tongue twisters or words that sound too much alike.
- Reading aloud helps create natural sounding dialogue.
- Watch for unnecessary dialogue. Even though it's clever and snappy, if a speech doesn't perform a function, you should cut it. Dialogue should add to character development, move the plot, or replace sections of narrative.

Ask Questions

As you revisit your dialogue, ask the following questions:

Am I telling instead of showing? Resist the urge to explain how your characters feel; writing is much more effective when it shows those feelings.

Telling: Paul was furious.

Showing: Paul threw his wine glass against the fireplace and the broken glass exploded across the hardwood floor.

Does the dialogue help establish each character's personality? Go over every conversation and see if you can find ways to show personality through speech and actions. However, don't give readers unnecessary information or cram too much into one speech. The following quote shows how John Sanford works a physical description into his novel, *Chosen Prey*. Having a character examine himself in a mirror is a cliché, but Sanford made it work because this action fits the character—a man who's excessively vain.

> He stood up, wobbled into the bathroom, flushed the Trojan in the toilet, washed perfunctorily, and studied himself in the mirror. Great eyes, he thought, suitably deep-set for a man of intellect. A good nose, trim, not fleshy. His pointed chin made his face into an oval, a reflection of sensitivity. He was admiring the image when his eyes drifted to the side of his nose: a whole series of small dark hairs were emerging from the line where his nose met his cheek. He *hated* that.

In this example we get a physical description from the character's viewpoint, and we know he thinks well of himself. Sanford builds this image of vanity throughout the book, but we later discover others see this character differently.

Are the nuts and bolts correct? Check quotation marks and other punctuation in your dialogue. It's easy to miss a quote, especially at the end of a sentence.

Have you used too many dialogue tags? Try to eliminate dialogue tags by using action and gestures to show who's speaking. Use "said" whenever possible, and avoid using adverbs in dialogue tags. Remember, people cannot snort, grimace, or laugh, while speaking.

Is the dialogue too long? Watch for passages that ramble for over half a page. If a character needs to say a lot, as in a courtroom summary, break the speech into sections by inserting text or letting other characters interrupt.

Are present participles correctly used? Words ending in *-ing* are useful dialogue tags, but make sure the actions described by the clauses can be performed at the same time. Don't overuse this device.

Have you used too much of a good thing? Some dialogue elements are easily overdone, so check for excessive use of:

- Italics: You *must* meet my brother, Henry."
- Exclamation points: Try not to use more than one per page.
- Profanity: Readers quickly get the point with profanity and swearing. No need to overdo it.
- Present participles: The *–ing* phrases become tiring for readers. Limit yourself to one or two per page.

Does each character have a voice? Unique speech patterns and phrasing should distinguish each character.

Do you tell readers what to think? If so, spend time on those passages and try substituting dialogue or action—guiding the reader without preaching. Each character's actions and decisions should present enough information so readers can form their own opinions.

Have you overused passive verbs? Although they usually aren't part of dialogue, passive verbs are my pet peeve, so I just had to work this in. Verbs such as: *was, were, would,* and *have* are passive because the action lacks a "doer." Locate passive verbs with the "find" function on your computer, or mark them with yellow as you review the manuscript. Limit yourself to only a few per page. The following statements are passive:

- The screen door was flapping in the breeze.
- John was running through the field, six feet ahead of the charging bull.

- They were standing in the doorway, just out of sight.

Now, let's make them active:

- The screen door flapped in the breeze.
- John tore through the field, a few desperate steps ahead of the charging bull.
- They lurked in the doorway out of sight.

Have you used contractions and realistic speech patterns? Sentence fragments are acceptable in dialogue, helping you keep it short, snappy, and interesting.

You may not enjoy the editing process, but it's an essential part of the writing craft. If you can't edit your own work, trade editing services with another writer, or better yet—hire a professional. If possible, let your manuscript cool for a few weeks before you begin the final edit. Starting another project before you reread the old one will enhance your objectivity.

Ten Quick and Easy Ways to Improve Your Dialogue

1. Show, don't tell. Always.
2. Keep dialogue tags short and simple. *Said* is the perfect tag.
3. Avoid talking heads by connecting dialogue to a scene.
4. Check and double check your punctuation and grammar.
5. Read your dialogue aloud.
6. Give each character a distinctive voice.
7. Each conversation should contain conflict, tension, or suspense. Every speaker needs a motive and a goal.
8. Use accents, dialects, and slang with care. A little goes a long way.
9. Use contractions so your speakers don't sound too formal.
10. Avoid long speeches—interspace them with action or narrative.

Notes

Bibliography

Bremen, Ellen, M.A. *Say This, NOT That to Your Professor: 36 Talking Tips for College Success.* NorLightsPress, 2012.

Bowen, Elizabeth. "Notes on Writing a Novel: An Essay" Narrative Magazine, Fall, 2006.

Carver, Raymond. *All of Us, The Collected Poems* Vintage; Reprint edition, 2000.

Connelly, Michael. *The Last Coyote.* Little, Brown and Company; 1st edition, 2003.

Dugoni, Robert. *The Jury Master.* Warner Books, 2006.

Dugoni, Robert. *Damage Control.* Grand Central Publishing, 2007.

Fitch, Janet. *White Oleander.* Little, Brown, & Company, 2001.

Fitzgerald, F. Scott. *The Great Gatsby.* Scribner; reissue edition, 2004.

Flinn, Denny Martin. *How Not to Write a Screenplay: 101 Common Mistakes Most Screenwriters Make.* Lone Eagle, 1999.

Gardner, Lisa. *Say Goodbye.* Bantam Dell. July, 2008.

Getz, Gin. *The Color of the Wild: An Intimate Look at Life in an Untamed Land.* NorLightsPress, 2014.

Grisham, John. *A Painted House.* Dell Publishing, 2001.

Hart, John. *The Last Child.* Minotaur Books. May, 2009.

Herriot, James. *All Creatures Great and Small.* St. Martin's Griffin. 2004.

Howey, Hugh. *WOOL.* Simon & Schuster, 2012.

King, Stephen. *On Writing: A Memoir of the Craft.* Pocket Books, 2000.

Kingsolver, Barbara. *Prodigal Summer.* Harper-Collins Publishers, 2001.

Lee, Harper. *To Kill a Mockingbird.* Little Brown & Company, re-issued 1998.

McCaffrey, Anne. *The Skies of Pern.* Del Rey, 2002.

Mullen, Jim. *It Takes a Village Idiot.* Simon & Schuster, 2001.

Roberts, Nora, *Montana Sky.* G. P. Putnam's Sons, 1996.

Ryan, P.B. *Still Life with Murder* (Nell Sweeney Mystery Series, Book 1), Berkely Prime Crime, 2003.

Sanford, John. *Chosen Prey,* Berkley, 2001.

Siddons, Anne Rivers. *Up Island.* HarperTorch, 1998.

Stein, Sol. *Six Points About Character, Plot, and Dialogue You Wish You'd Known Yesterday.* Writer's Store. www.writersstore.com.

Stockton, Shreve. *The Daily Coyote: A Story of Love, Survival, and Trust in the Wilds of Wyoming.* Simon & Schuster, 2008.

Stowe, Harriet Beecher. *Uncle Tom's Cabin.* Simon & Brown, March, 2012 (reprint).

Wallace, Bill. *The Christmas Spurs.* Pocket Books, 1990.

White, Steven. *The Program*. Dell, 2002.

Willems, Mo. Interview with Jill Martin Wrenn, "Jealousy, Joy, and Driving a Bus: The Secrets to Writing a Hit Children's Book." http://www.cnn.com/2013/04/23/living/books-mo-willems/.

Wingate, Molly, M.A., Woodward, Marty, M.S. *Slow Parenting Teens: How to Create a Positive, Respectful, and Fun Relationship with your Teenager.* NorLightsPress, 2012.

Wingfield, R. D. *Night Frost*. Bantam Books, 1992.

Index

CPSIA information can be obtained at www.ICGtesting.com
Printed in the USA
BVOW08s0126170614

356585BV00007B/38/P